"The principal lessons of this hilarious book are: (1) you know more than you think you do, and (2) the so-called experts know less. *Why Nobody Believes the Numbers* shows how a little fifth-grade arithmetic can invalidate much of what passes for outcomes."

—Regina Herzlinger
Nancy R. McPherson Professor of Business Administration,
Harvard Business School

"*Why Nobody Believes the Numbers* exposes the poor design and invalid statistics of disease-management programs in a credible, user-friendly fashion. The case studies and mathematical proofs show readers how to identify and address outcome measurement malpractice. Its entertaining style can keep readers' interest long after they might otherwise have closed the book on the statistical fallacies of study design."

—Nancy Kane
Professor of Management and Associate Dean
for Educational Programs,
Harvard School of Public Health

"*Why Nobody Believes the Numbers* is an amusing but incisive look at vendor outcomes numbers that don't even come close to adding up and yet are widely accepted. I'd recommend this book to all CFOs and HR executives who want to improve the health of their members but do it cost-effectively."

—Dean Karlan
Professor of Economics, Yale University;
Founder, StickK.com

"Only someone like Al Lewis, who has mastered a complex field like outcomes measurement for disease management programs, could write a book that is so funny and so much fun, while being so enlightening."

—James Prochaska
Founder of Pro-Change Behavior Systems, Inc.

"Al Lewis is not only the 'inventor of disease management.' He is also smarter than a fifth grader, who in turn is apparently smarter than most consultants and vendors in this field. Much of outcomes measurement is like Las Vegas: you know you are getting taken, but you visit anyway. *Why Nobody Believes the Numbers* explains how you are being bamboozled by the croupiers of the population health management industry. Caveat emptor no more!"

—Dave Rearick, DO
Vice President of Medical Management, Marsh & McLennan

"Lewis sugarcoats the bitter medicine of math with a generous amount of humor, making this the most painless lesson in outcomes analysis ever published. The lesson: trust your own judgment. If you are smarter than a fifth grader, you can determine whether your programs save money."

—Tom Scully
Administrator, Centers for Medicare and Medicaid
Services (2001–2003);
Senior Counsel, Alston & Bird;
Partner, Welsh Carson, Anderson & Stowe

"I don't recall fifth-grade math being this funny. But apparently a lot of vendors and consultants don't recall it at all."

—William H. Tobey
Senior Fellow, Belfer Center, Harvard University

"Lewis has singlehandedly created what industry committees have failed to create: a how-to guide for valid outcomes analysis to support vendors, employers, consultants, and carriers. It could even be a textbook for Master's in Health Administration programs, except it is too much fun to read."

—Warren Todd
President and Executive Director,
Care Continuum Alliance (2001–2006)

"*Why Nobody Believes the Numbers* explores hilarious case studies of vendors and health plans whose THC-induced ROI calculations violate every rule of arithmetic, rules that the author notes must be strictly enforced. The book then offers some practical advice on contracting and measurement that if followed would enhance the field's credibility and long-range growth prospects."

—Tom Underwood
CEO, Sandata Technologies;
CEO, Alere Health (2010–2012)

WHY
NOBODY
BELIEVES
THE
NUMBERS

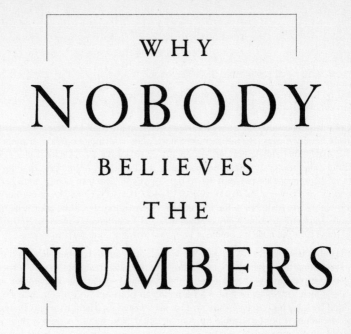

WHY
NOBODY
BELIEVES
THE
NUMBERS

DISTINGUISHING
FACT FROM FICTION

in

POPULATION HEALTH
MANAGEMENT

A L   L E W I S

WILEY

John Wiley & Sons, Inc.

Published by John Wiley & Sons, Inc., Hoboken, New Jersey.
Published simultaneously in Canada.

For general information on our other products and services or for technical support, please contact our Customer Care Department within the United States at (800) 762-2974, outside the United States at (317) 572-3993 or fax (317) 572-4002.

Wiley publishes in a variety of print and electronic formats and by print-on-demand. Some material included with standard print versions of this book may not be included in e-books or in print-on-demand. If this book refers to media such as a CD or DVD that is not included in the version you purchased, you may download this material at http://booksupport.wiley.com. For more information about Wiley products, visit www.wiley.com.

Library of Congress Cataloging-in-Publication Data:

Lewis, Al
  Why nobody believes the numbers : distinguishing fact from fiction in population health management / Al Lewis.
      p. cm.
  ISBN 978-1-118-31318-3 (hardback); ISBN 978-1-118-33536-9 (ebk); ISBN 978-1-118-33420-1 (ebk); ISBN 978-1-118-33206-1 (ebk)
  1. Health maintenance organizations–Evaluation–United States. 2. Managed care plans (Medical care)–Standards–United States. I. Title.
    RA413.5.U5L49 2012
    362.1'042584–dc23

                                                                              2012003575

Printed in the United States of America.

10 9 8 7 6 5 4 3 2

To my fifth-grade math teacher, for doing a better job than the other kids' fifth-grade math teachers.

Contents

Introduction

This book contains arithmetic. DON'T HIT ME. However, I promise that the arithmetic will be quite accessible, even to people who say they "can't do math." Oh, and you think you can't do math? You'll see examples of vendors and consultants whose math skills couldn't land them a job as the "before" picture on *Sesame Street*.

This promise is possible partly because *Why Nobody Believes the Numbers* largely avoids things that make other books about numbers real turn-offs, such as, for example, numbers. But mostly it's possible because I am a great writer. Don't take my word for it—just look at the evidence:

- I am blessed with such effective persuasive powers that I was once able, against all odds, to convince a resort to sell me a timeshare.
- My first book got eight five-star reviews on Amazon, including four from people I don't even recall having slept with.

The bottom line: The math is presented clearly enough that readers who understand it can probably continue to live independently for at least a few more years.

Now that we've settled that issue, let's review what you probably already know if you've bought this book, or borrowed it from a friend

temporarily until your own copy(ies) arrive in the mail: Vendors*
routinely show you outcomes reports for your Population Health
Improvement** programs whose savings claims are much closer to
fiction than fact.

But you don't know *why* these numbers are fictional, do you?
You leaf through these vendor outcomes reports, squint thought-
fully, and then ask your vendor's account manager: "Did you control
for regression to the mean?" In response, the vendor will babble
something about how their methodology is Extremely Scientific, so,
of course, it "adjusts" for regression to the mean. Plus, their methodology is "validated" by [fill in the name of an actuarial firm that will
happily put their name on anything if you pay them enough money],
so obviously the resulting savings estimate is accurate because a real
actuary says it is.

You nod your head, and that's the end of the conversation.
Vendor 1, Customer 0.

It's like the time I took my car to the auto mechanic because
it was making a funny noise. We raised the hood. As we listened
to the engine idling, I rubbed my chin and nodded knowledgeably.
Then, I diagnosed the problem *right on the spot*, just to make sure
this shyster wouldn't think he could take advantage of me.

I said, "I think it's time to replace the distributor caps," only to
be informed by this particular shyster that this particular problem
was unlikely to be distributor caps, because this particular car didn't
have distributor caps.

Lacking any knowledge of what a distributor cap does, whether
distributor caps are or ever were found in cars, or for that matter
how any car not driven by Fred Flintstone actually gets around, I

---

*Or carrier. Unless otherwise indicated in this book or obvious from the context,
a *vendor* is any organization, whether independent or carrier-affiliated, that sells a
program where outcomes need to be measured. Whether the vendors in question
are independent or carrier-affiliated is indicated in their code names, like *Vendor A*
or *Health Plan C*.

**PHI encompasses all programs designed to save money by improving health or
access to care. See the Glossary for a full definition of this term and others used in
this book.

had no alternative but to take his word for that conclusion, as well as everything else he told me when he presented the bill. He could have told me that spiders had built webs in the canister valve and I would have believed him. Come to think of it, that's what he *did* tell me.*

And, that, my friends, is roughly what happens in Population Health Improvement just about every time you read a proposal, negotiate a contract, or review an outcomes report. This assertion covers disease management, medical homes, value-based contracting, productivity/absenteeism management, on-site clinics, and *especially* wellness. (Wellness is five years behind disease management in measurement, which is like being five years behind Iraq in democracy.) Just like the mechanic with the arachnid-infested canister valve, vendors can tell you whatever they want because you don't know what you're doing and they know it.

This isn't your fault. For starters, you have an *actual day job*. You've got tons of other things to worry about, whereas vendors have entire staffs whose job is to find new ways to rip you off. You think I'm kidding? We have a dozen vignettes and case studies of vendors performing math-defying feats, in one case making costs disappear even before the program starts.

Second, you have benefits consultants (or, in the case of health plans, actuaries) whose job it is to analyze this stuff and make sense of it for you. Well, guess what: Your consultants are every bit as ignorant as you are. Once again, if you think I'm kidding, wait 'til you read about some of their misdeeds. Worse, they get paid much more than you do, to the tune of $500/hour, to understand outcomes math, and they still don't. Only two benefits consultants have ever achieved Critical Outcomes Report Analysis certification—and yet, here's what benefits consultants do for a living: critically analyze outcomes reports.

---

*That really is what he told me. Apparently spiders are so attracted to canister valves in Acuras that the fix is provided free. I am not a vendor so nothing in this book is made up.

Why Does the Author Hate Benefits Consultants?

Some of the references to benefits consultants in this book are not flattering. You might ask: "Why does the author hate benefits consultants? When he was a kid, was he bitten by one?"

Quite the contrary: (a) I don't hate benefits consultants, and (b) despite years of therapy, any memory of being bitten by one remains repressed. Paradoxically, I get a large number of referrals from benefits consultants. And I think, based on the side-by-side consulting that I've done with them, benefits consultants excel at the following:

1. Benefits consulting

However, I also think, based on the data I've seen, that they are quite bad at the following:

2. Everything else*

A "health benefit" is something that you automatically get as part of your health insurance, like covered drugs, a certain number of visits to the chiropractor, and so forth. When you use those services, you fill out a claim, usually pay a co-pay, and get reimbursed for the rest. Figuring out how to design a benefits structure to control spending while keeping employees happy, and picking a carrier to do that, is the role of the benefits consultant. Many do it very well. Some of the best at those activities, knowing that what they are being asked to measure or procure is not the same as what they are expert at, will call me or someone like me in to work side-by-side with them on...

...Population Health Improvement (PHI), which this book is about. PHI does not fit in the statutory category of

---

*And the reverse is true, too. No one would ever want me doing benefits consulting for him or her. I would have no clue, for instance, how to estimate the effect of a change in drug co-pay levels on total health spending. I'm not an actuary. I don't even play one on TV.

"health benefits" and therefore is not something that benefits consultants automatically know how to procure or measure. PHI consists of administrative programs designed to reduce the need for benefits by making people healthier on a large scale. There are no claims forms—and certainly no co-pays. The tools that these consultants learned in actuarial charm school to analyze benefits spending do not apply to PHI, though that doesn't stop them from using these tools, often with hilarious results, as case study after case study will show.

They prefer to spend their (highly billable) time writing overwrought, uber-detailed requests for proposals and/or contracts dictating every conceivable contingency in the life of a disease manager—from what to do following a specified number of unsuccessful attempts to contact patients/employees by phone to what to do in the event of being sexually harassed by a presidential candidate.

Instead, perhaps they should use their time adopting the specific tools to understand and measure PHI, which are right in this very book, and, as one might conclude from the case studies, apparently nowhere else. So if your consultant is reading this book and especially if he is sharing his copy with you, chances are you've found one willing to learn how to analyze PHI.

It's also possible they've picked this stuff up through osmosis. If so, that would be reflected in their ability to negotiate a contract and measure an outcome. You can check this yourselves by reading the last chapter to see if your contract(s) for PHI are well-negotiated or your outcomes reports well-vetted.

Perhaps people don't think they have to critically analyze outcomes reports, because their trade association has done that for them. Vendors will often say: "Our ROI methodology follows the Care Continuum Alliance (CCA) Outcomes Guidelines." Unfortunately, the industry pre-post methodology section of the CCA Outcomes Guidelines is built on a completely invalid premise. The premise is, as the first chapter will show, mathematically not just questionable, but also provably wrong—and you will also see that another methodology is provably right. To the CCA's credit, they don't even *pretend* that their guidelines are based on provable math. Instead, they call them "consensus guidelines."*

This is a critical hedge: Unlike sociology or philosophy or global warming, real math is not consensus-based. Maybe if you're Dunder Mifflin's Michael G. Scott it is. ("Why does 2 + 2 = 4? Because everybody agrees that it should, that's why.") But for the rest of us, math is *proof*-based. Numbers either add up or they don't. There are not multiple ways of doing math leading to different answers. 2 + 2 = 4, period. Suppose you ask your banker how much money is in your bank account. Your banker doesn't say: "Well, it depends on how you measure. There are different methodologies." You'll see for yourself in Chapter 1 ("Actuaries Behaving Badly") that the vendor-endorsed "industry consensus" measurement of today will always overstate savings.

Then, because this isn't a mystery book, I won't leave you hanging until the end to learn that indeed you *can* measure outcomes validly using proof rather than consensus. While the actual, mathematically correct, way to measure outcomes is a bit cumbersome, the good news is that …

… Chapter 2 ("How to Measure Outcomes Using Ingredients You Already Have in Your Kitchen") presents an ersatz measurement proxy that can be estimated without math, using observational data to figure out whether you are "moving the needle" or not. Instead of math, there are a bunch of graphs. This means that, in the immortal words of the great philosopher Yogi Berra, you can observe a lot just by watching. And that's what Chapter 2 is about. Observational data is used to create "plausibility tests." You look at actual event

---

*Oscar Wilde noted that there is no need to cheat if you hold the winning cards, so full disclosure: The CCA emphasizes on page 34 of their guidelines that their consensus methodology, even with their many adjustments (a list that somehow leaves out the adjustment suggested in *Why Nobody Believes* that would actually give their methodology a shot at being valid) do not approach the accuracy of a true randomized controlled trial (RCT). If you could do RCTs in the real world, you'd probably get the numbers right, but half of your members would be pretty miffed at you, which is why few payors ever do them.

rates over time (heart attacks, asthma attacks, and so forth) and ask whether the return-on-investment (ROI) that the vendor is insisting you received is plausible given the changes in event rates over time in your population. Plausibility-checking turns out to be easy, fast, and inexpensive, as well as valid, which is probably why most vendors don't do it, consultants pretend they've never heard of it, and the CCA doesn't emphasize it.

You don't learn to drive just by reading a book on driving, and you don't learn to apply plausibility tests just by reading a chapter on them. Instead, your next step in learning to drive is to watch someone do it, badly. "Badly" because engineers say you learn more from one bridge that falls down than from 100 that stay up. In this industry, the ratio is almost the reverse, and that's what Chapters 3 and 4 are all about: Short vignettes and longer case studies--involving disease management, wellness, patient-centered medical homes, and more—of vendors who, analytically speaking, drive drunk. Examples of real companies—possibly including even your own vendor—caught either flunking plausibility tests or simply making up numbers. These examples aren't obscure outcomes reports that we discovered by hacking into someone's voicemail like Rupert Murdoch. In most cases, these violations are *right on the vendor's own websites* or right in their brochures. It's as if they are daring you to challenge their numbers—and the examples of vendors bragging about their phony numbers epitomize the complete lack of respect that vendors have for you and your consultants.

Yes, it's true: These companies, carriers, and even states eagerly broadcast their math-defying fantasies with breathless albeit misplaced enthusiasm. One vendor, which we will call Vendor A, used a mass e-mail to proclaim some mathematically impossible results, and urged people to share them. I wrote back and said that I'd happily share those results, as an example of how not to analyze outcomes. The CEO wrote back and said: "I want to be VERY clear that the study summary that you received from Vendor A was part of a transmittal to our 'Friends of Vendor A' e-mail list. As such, it was not sent to you as a publication or marketing claim, and should not be used by you for any purpose other than to provide feedback to us directly."

I wrote back and said: "If this was private, you shouldn't have posted it on your website." Then the CEO wrote: "A published, peer-reviewed article is coming soon. Stay tuned!" Almost as if on cue, the *New England Journal of Medicine* shortly thereafter published a research article showing that utilization reduction using the Vendor A system was *79 percentage points lower* than Vendor A's claim.

Vendor A is a perfect example: *Why Nobody Believes the Numbers* kicks posterior and take appellations. If someone from one of the vendors in a case study wants to sue, perhaps on the grounds that their name really is Vendor A, I say, "If you sue me, you'll have to sue Newton, Descartes, Pythagorus, and all their buddies, because this isn't about name-calling or accusations. This is about fifth-grade math, and apparently the only thing you know about fifth-grade math is that you can't do it." I can, however. I guarantee it: If any reader can find an invalidating flaw in the math before June 2013, not only will I at my own expense refund your purchase price, but I will even let you still keep the book. That's the kind of warm-hearted, magnanimous guy I am. Plus, I don't want your germs.

The three subsequent chapters—5 through 8 for those of you keeping score at home—show that it is indeed possible to procure a contract that guarantees valid savings, and have the vendor deliver on those savings. These case studies saved money, for real. The vendors did their job well enough to show savings even though the measurement was valid.

By the way, those of you keeping score at home need to pay a little bit more attention, even if it means putting down your brewskis for a minute: "5 through 8" is four chapters, not three. It's actually Chapters 5 through 7 that have the case studies. And therein lies my point: Most people will simply accept the math that they read. *Why Nobody Believes* counsels the opposite: Check every piece of arithmetic you see because in this field most calculations are wrong, often to the point of being impossible.

Finally, in Chapter 8, you'll be able to synthesize all these insights into a contract or request for proposal (RFP) that lets prospective vendors know that you weren't born yesterday, and that sneaking a phony outcome past you would be like sneaking a Senator past a lobbyist.

Once you've finished *Why Nobody Believes*, you'll find that the math is nowhere near as complex as your vendors and consultants make it out to be. Your job will become much easier. True, it still won't be the world's easiest job. That would be: Pip, where the entire job description consists of repeating what Gladys Knight says and occasionally adding train noises.

You'll find the Pips *apropos* for another reason, too: When you identify your first measurement fallacy, you'll want to jump up from your chair and shout: "Whoo-whoo!"

Chapter 1

Actuaries Behaving Badly

L et's start by exploring the validity of the most popular pre-post guidelines, as compared to another much less publicized methodology. By then attempting to prove each, we'll learn, in the immortal words of the great philosopher Rick Perry, whether or not who is right.

Some Background: We're Shocked, Shocked, to Find That Invalidity Is Going On in Here

Many people in the care management field complain that nobody believes their numbers. It turns out there's a reason for that: The numbers are mostly made up. I say this with great regret. First, because my job—helping buyers with analysis and procurement—would be much more satisfying if I could deliver good news. Like an East German border guard told the *New York Times* shortly after he was told he could open his gate: "My job is much more fun now that I can let people through instead of shooting them."

Second, the methodology that is at the heart of the fallacies was invented by someone I know well and trust innately—me. Yep, I invented the pre-post methodology I'm about to blow up. Really. You can google "invented disease management" if you like. If you mention pre-post to real biostatisticians, they'll laugh at you. Look in any public health graduate school course catalog under "biostatistics" and you won't see any reference to pre-post methodologies in the course catalog. The pharmaceutical industry discarded the idea of pre-post as a valid measurement tool almost a century ago, about the same time they stopped experimenting on prisoners. (Ironically, there is at least one disease management program involving prisoners.) The idea of measuring outcomes using a pre-post methodology is so thoroughly discredited in health services research that there wasn't even a book about it until this one, for the simple reason that until the population health improvement field came along, nobody did it.

So, why did population health improvement re-introduce this concept? Two reasons. First, no one—including me, at first—knew any better. Literally, there are only two people prominent in this field with the requisite background for studying population health improvement as though it were an actual academically sound discipline, and at least one of them has pretty much given up on crying in the wilderness.*

Second, when implementing population health improvement programs, few health plans or self-insured employers are willing to deny enrollment to some of their members or employees in order to create a control group getting no intervention, the gold standard for study design. It's not even clear that it is legal under governing law to deny some people an intervention made available to others.

As a result, pre-post study designs covering the entire relevant population have become the norm. Two pre-post methods are in popular use:

- *Prospective Identification*: In this "once chronic, always chronic" methodology favored by many vendors and consultants, a member added to the disease population in any period remains in the disease population in future periods

---

*Ariel Linden is his name. He has published extensively in this field. He can be reached at alinden@lindenconsulting.org. The other is Ron Goetzel, who will be cited later.

even if the member incurs no disease-related claims in those subsequent periods.

◆ *Annual Requalification*: Some consultants prefer this methodology, as does The Care Continuum Alliance/CCA. Unlike the prospective identification method, individuals must be re-identified annually through claims data to be counted as disease members in that year.

Both methods embody the consensus of many industry stakeholders. Unfortunately, the consensus pre-post methodology, in all its permutations used to calculate financial outcomes for population-based disease management and wellness programs, lacks the slightest foundation in math.

No matter how strong the consensus, math is not a popularity contest. For instance, the majority of Americans believes that the majority of the 9/11 terrorists were Iraqis. However, none of the 9/11 terrorists were Iraqis. The math trumps the consensus.

During the 15 years in which pre-post designs have been in use by consensus, no one has even attempted to prove the validity of pre-post measurement, which is a good thing because if they tried, they would find exactly the opposite: The attempt to prove that pre-post is valid would result in proving it to be invalid. Nonetheless, most of the industry's vendors and consultants accept the CCA consensus guidelines more or less on faith. And the rest of this chapter is about why that faith is misplaced: The major premise of the CCA guidelines is simply wrong. (The proof will refer occasionally to the CCA Outcomes Guidelines as short-hand for their pre-past methodology. The CCA Outcomes Guidelines cover many methodologies and recommend where possible prospective controlled trials, such as the HealthDialog example in Chapter 7, but cover pre-post in great detail only because that's the methodology most vendors and consultants use.)

The CCA says it does not endorse pre-post (recommending more rigorous methodologies where practical), but rather merely codifies the way consultants and vendors use it. Hence, this section is not a knock against the CCA itself, which claims it is agnostic about the results. They merely provided the forum for a 50-person

Outcomes Guidelines Committee to agree, and occasionally we will use the abbreviation CCA to refer to that group. Since this committee contained no formal hierarchy, everyone's opinions had to be taken into consideration—so perhaps it is possible that the people with the most to lose by valid measurement had the loudest opinions.

How would we know if that's the case? Well, half of me (the half that is convinced there was a second gunman on the grassy knoll) says the CCA knows the major premise is wrong and just put these consensus guidelines out there because they subtly overstate savings most of the time.

The other half of me (the half that thinks, nah, if there had been a conspiracy among the Mafia, the CIA, Lyndon Johnson, and for good measure let's throw in Fidel Castro, someone would have ratted them out by now) says that the CCA is a very well-intentioned organization that recruited the most dedicated volunteers in the industry, who then spent untold hours on conference calls, and tried their hardest to develop an accurate methodology. Unfortunately, the outcomes committee being comprised mostly of people trained in healthcare, they simply missed the mark on the math. An honest mistake.

Which is it—an honest mistake or an attempt to overstate savings? The next edition of the Outcomes Guidelines will answer that question: If the CCA's Committee, having now read this chapter, switches from invalid consensus methodologies to valid proof-based methodologies in the section covering pre-post, then Oswald acted alone.

Why are we picking on the CCA's guidelines? Is it because its authors are dumber than everyone else? No, it's because they're smarter than everyone else, and are the only ones willing to publish their guidelines—free, no less. People who don't use their guidelines would actually be upgrading if they did. If some of the benefits consulting and brokerage firms were to publish their guidelines, a book alone wouldn't do them justice. They'd need a mascot, like "Crime Dog" Fred MacRuff, with a slogan like: "Take a Bite Out of Claims. Let's Reduce Them by More Than 100%."

Want a sense of the level of mathematical sophistication for people who aren't using CCA guidelines? Here's an actual exchange between me and someone who was using individual patients as their own control, an antediluvian methodology whose merits, such as they are, will be extinguished in Chapter 2, a methodology even the CCA Guidelines dismiss. A salesperson was showing my clients and me case studies of her firm's interventions in complex cases, each one resulting in dramatic savings. (It is, as we will see, virtually impossible not to show savings in complex cases—which, as a group, decline in cost after the sentinel events that earned them designation as complex cases take place—intervention or no intervention.)

Case study after case study showing these savings went up on the screen. I asked, politely at first but then with increasing frustration, what the average savings was across these cases. No luck—the case studies continued unabated. Finally, I offered to simply exit the meeting and come back when the presenter was ready to tell us the average. At that point the presenter addressed the issue, albeit in an exasperated tone of voice suggesting that only a complete imbecile could possibly think my question was a good one.

"There is no average," she replied. "It varies."

The Proof: Doing the Pre-Post Math for Grown-Ups

In school, "proof" was a scary word. It also involved a lot of other scary words, like "axiom" and "theorem" and "cosine" and even occasionally "scalene." And, yes, I know we promised that we would only use fifth-grade math in our proofs and case studies, but we lied. It turns out that proving the invalidity of pre-post methodologies requires only *fourth*-grade math.

The validity of both the annual and prospective pre-post methodologies requires identifying the complete "disease population." The fact that many members are not identifiable as "disease members" necessarily creates invalid outcomes, no matter which of the two popular pre-post methodologies is used.

Why Might a Disease Member not be Identifiable to a DM Program in the Baseline?

1. The member's condition is too mild to trigger the algorithm, which normally requires a certain minimum number of prescription fills or diagnosis codes.
2. The member, though diagnosed, is new to the health plan.
3. The member is undiagnosed.
4. The member is noncompliant.
5. The member is misdiagnosed.
6. The member is correctly diagnosed, but as part of a periodic preventive physical, and the physician codes for the physical, not the diagnosis.
7. The member got diagnosed too recently for the claim to have shown up in the data warehouse.
8. The member fills prescriptions using a low-cost generic program, such as Wal-Mart's, and doesn't generate a claim.
9. The member belongs to a culture where having a diagnosis is frowned upon.

We're now going to run a set of tables, simplifying the discussion so that a payor only has two asthmatics.

Consider first the following table. *Prospective identification* (once chronic, always chronic) counts everyone ever identified with the disease from the point of identification going forward. *Annual requalification* counts as disease members only people who trigger the disease algorithm every year. Therefore, Asthmatic #1, who clearly has asthma (having had a $2,000 asthma inpatient event in 2010), gets counted in 2011 only with prospective identification, not annual requalification. The counting strategy yields an obviously incorrect 2011 program outcome for prospective identification. The stated outcome for annual requalification reveals the reality that the year-over-year change in cost is indeed $0.

Person	2010 Costs	2011 Costs	Change in Costs
Asthmatic #1	$2,000	$0 (invisible in annual requalification)	
Asthmatic #2	$0 (Invisible)	$2,000	
Cost per Asthmatic—Prospective Identification Method	*$2,000*	*$1,000*	*−50%*
Cost per Asthmatic—Annual Requalification Method	*$2,000*	*$2,000*	*0*
Actual Cost per Asthmatic	*$1,000*	*$1,000*	*0*

However—and a quirk like this should be a red flag in a demonstration of validity—even though the year-over-year difference is accurately portrayed in annual requalification, the arithmetic average cost per asthmatic itself is overstated by a factor of two ($2,000 versus $1,000).

In another, more common real-world example, assume that Asthmatic #1 decided to control his asthma after his attack by filling $200 worth of prescriptions in 2011. This restates the claims pattern—and distorts the answer—as follows:

Person	2010	2011	Change in Costs
Asthmatic #1	$2,000	$200	
Asthmatic #2	$0 (Invisible)	$2,000	
Cost per Asthmatic—Prospective Identification Method	*$2,000*	*$1,100*	*−45%*
Cost per Asthmatic—Annual Requalification Method	*$2,000*	*$1,100*	*−45%*
Actual Cost per Asthmatic	*$1,000*	*$1,100*	*+10%*

Annual requalification shows a 45 percent reduction in costs per asthmatic, *even as the overall total claims paid climbed 10 percent ($2,000 to $2,200)!* Although this hypothetical could be criticized as an asymmetrical example designed specifically to invalidate the methodology (with more than a modicum of success, I might add), in real life asymmetry is the rule, not the exception: Members are more likely to comply with medication after an attack than before an attack. Therefore, a drug claim is more likely to show up after an attack than before an attack. If the likelihood of an attack was not affected by drug use, making the example symmetrical, the implication would be that drug use would not be valuable in preventing attacks. That is why the more realistic examples would show more drugspend following attacks than preceding them.

Besides, a mathematically valid methodology would work with any claims pattern, symmetrical or not. If something is proven valid, there are no exceptions. Remember the $a^2 + b^2 = c^2$ thing (the Pythagorean Theorem) you learned in sixth grade? It turns out that the equation works with integers only when you square them. There is no set of three integers where you can cube the smaller two integers to sum to the largest one cubed. Further, it turns out that it's not just cubing that's impossible: there is no power and no three integers where raising the two smaller of the three integers to that power equals the third integer raised to that same power. This is Fermat's Last Theorem. It was tested and tested up to extremely high exponents with no exceptions being found. Nonetheless, this Theorem wasn't *proven* until someone showed that no exceptions *could* be found. One exception would have invalidated that Theorem, but now it's a proof.

By contrast, not only do tons of exceptions invalidate the common pre-post methodologies, but it's actually pretty darn hard to find any combination of real-world numbers that support it.

Adding Asthmatic #2 to the disease population will exacerbate the savings misstatement because he gets added only *after* his high-cost sentinel event

Often a member is triggered for entry into the disease population by having an expensive health event. However, adding a person to a cohort once he has presented with a disease—meaning *after* his costs have already increased, or during the year in which his costs increased—overstates savings. Although the increase in his costs from the prior year doesn't get attributed to the program, his subsequent decline in costs does get attributed to the program. Consider the course of disease in Asthmatic #2:

	2010 (Baseline)	2011 (Contract Year 1)	2012 (Contract Year 2)
Status	Not in population	Added to population in year of event "trigger"	In population
Asthmatic #2's costs	$0	$2,000	$200
Cost or savings (vs. prior year) attributed to the DM program using either methodology	*N/A*	*$0*	*−$1,800 (savings)*
Summary of Asthmatic #2's impact on savings (2011–2012)			*2011–2012 program savings is increased by $1,800*

Somehow, $1,800 was shown as savings between 2010 and 2012, even though Asthmatic #2's costs per year *increased* by a net amount of $200 from the 2010 to 2012 period. When a vendor or consultant explains, "People are added to the baseline as soon as they are identified with the condition," they mean that there is no mathematical recognition of the baseline experience preceding the sentinel event leading to the identification. To count savings starting with the sentinel event or incident (or the year in which the sentinel incident took place) creates only the illusion of savings. If the accounting shows a year-over-year savings between 2011 and

2012, it must show a loss between 2010 and 2011 in order to capture the reality of the $200 increase in the annual cost for that asthmatic over the full three-year period.*

This fallacy of including people in the measured cohort only after they show up as being high cost or high risk, is even more common in wellness than in disease management. Consider this quotation from a corporate medical director in the *Wall Street Journal* health blog of July 29, 2010: "The same people [lose weight] every year. They get paid for it. They gain weight back. They lose it again. They get paid again." Overstating program success is inevitable.

This dynamic allows some health plans and wellness organizations to claim progress even when there is none. We'll show several examples of this, most notably Health Plan B's wellness program, which has elevated this dynamic to an art form.**

This Vendor A/Health Plan B stuff is very annoying. Can't you simply tell us the real names of the vendors and health plans in the case studies?

Three answers to that question:

 1. Sure.
 2. Any time.
 3. We take Amex, Mastercard, and Visa.

---

*Most vendors and actuarial consultants prefer to do all calculations in dollars, even though (1) unit cost is not affected by DM or wellness, just the number of units; (2) doing everything in dollars discourages people from checking to see if units actually declined where they were supposed to decline, such as days of care, and increased where they should have increased, such as preventive drug use. I strongly prefer doing everything in units and am writing largely in dollar terms only to "speak the language" of most readers.

** *Why Nobody Believes the Numbers* is about fact, not opinion, so we mean this observation literally, not figuratively. Health Plan A has literally made math into an art form in its bar graphs—see Chapter 4.

Yes, it's true: You need to *pay* for that information (as well as links to the original charts and other information that can't be published due to copyright restrictions) with a separate $29 purchase on www.dismgmt.com. There are several reasons for this. First, in the very unlikely chance that a vendor or carrier changes their offering and measurement to make their results valid, we want to know exactly who received the information about the original invalidity with the vendor's name, so that we can notify them. Second, if there is any other correction to the book needed over time, we can let you know. Third, I have to make some money somewhere. You don't seriously think I'm making any money writing this book, do you? Do the math on the royalties and compare that to the hours and hours of my free time it took to write this thing. I had to forego an entire season of *Survivor*. For all I know a contestant finally got bitten by a snake and I missed it.

USING THE TREND OF THE NON-CHRONIC POPULATION AS A PROXY FOR THE CHRONIC POPULATION WILL OVERSTATE SAVINGS

The consensus methodologies call for an inflation adjustment. Often, if not always, that adjustment is the trend in the non-chronic population. The CCA, constrained by the voluntary nature of the committee structure to crowdsource everyone's opinions about how they'd like the arithmetic to turn out, is naturally right at the forefront of this scheme, insisting on using at least some of the non-chronic trend with ***bold italics***, just in case anyone has a neurological condition that prevents regular print from penetrating that portion of their brain responsible for making dumb decisions:

> *CCA recommends the use of a non-chronic population to calculate this trend ... defined as those members not identified as having ... diabetes, CAD, heart failure, asthma [and/or] COPD.*

The Guidelines then add:

> *CCA further recommends use of the average historical dif-*
> *ference in chronic trend and non-chronic trend to adjust*
> *current year trend.**

I'm not sure what the second sentence means, except that the CCA required me to put it in, before they would give permission to reprint the first sentence. Whatever it is, it's not math. Math textbooks don't contain the word "historical." The fifth-grade arithmetic app on your smartphone doesn't include a "compromise" feature that automatically averages two completely different solutions to the same problem. Averaging two solutions reduces your odds of a right answer from a possible 50 percent to a certain 0 percent. It would be like an atheist and a fundamentalist compromising that every other word in the Bible is true.

I don't know what predicts the chronic trend (and in the discussion of valid methodologies, you'll see that you don't have to bother trying), but it's not the non-chronic people who happen to have been findable for some vaguely historical period. As you'll see below, whether you rely on the non-chronic population to supply half your trend or all of your trend or some other random proportion of your trend, and no matter what historical period you look at, it's wrong.

For the non-chronic calculation of trend to be valid, two things must be the case, neither of which is. First, the epidemiology must work: There must be such a thing as a non-chronic population that can be separated from the chronic population. Second, the arithmetic must work out so that, if it is possible to separate the two populations, claims trends in the real world are similar in both populations.

Unfortunately, neither the epidemiology nor the arithmetic withstands the slightest scrutiny.

---

*Care Continuum Alliance, *Outcomes Guidelines* Volume 5, 71, www.carecontinuum .org. In fairness to the CCA, *all* of their recommendations are in boldface italics, not just the dumb ones.

To Paraphrase the Immortal Words of the Great Philosopher Dinah Washington, What a Difference a Trend Makes

Like hanging chads, a slight tweak in trend assumptions could swing the entire financial outcome from positive to negative (or vice-versa).

In this real-life example Table 1.1, note that the savings percentage (3 percent) is far less than the assumed trend factor (21 percent). Building in a 21 percent trend factor changes the calculation from a large loss to a 3 percent gain, meaning

TABLE 1.1 Sensitivity of Savings Calculations to Trend

Baseline Year	All Conditions
Disease-Member Months	150,000
Claims Costs	$50,000,000
Exclusions/Stop Loss (claims in excess of $100,000/person)	$1,300,000
Net Claims Costs (after taking out excluded costs)	$48,700,000
Baseline Per-Disease-Member-Per-Month Costs	$325
Contract Year 3	
Disease-Member Months	169,000
Claims Costs	$68,000,000
Exclusions/Stop Loss (claims in excess of $100,000/person)	$3,200,000
Net Claims Costs (after taking out excluded costs)	$64,800,000
Contract Year 3 Per-Disease-Member-Per-Month Costs	$383
Contractual Inflation Trend Adjustment	21%
Baseline Per-Disease-Member-Per-Month Costs Adjusted for Trend	$394
Baseline Claims Costs Overall, Adjusted for Trend	$64,154,439
Savings	**$2,354,438.65**
Increase in Claims Costs Before Trend Adjustment (%)	**18%**
Reduction in Claims Costs After Trend Adjustment (%)	**3%**
Reduction in Claims Costs After Trend Adjusted ($)	**$11**

(*continued*)

(*continued*)

that a mere three-point decrease in the trend assumption would reduce the savings to zero. And even a one-point decrease in trend assumption—from 21 percent to 20 percent—would reduce the savings by a third (3 percent to 2 percent).

Those with a discerning eye will also notice that the "exclusions/stop-loss" claims removed from the calculation altogether more than double between the two periods. Had there been no high-cost claims exclusion, even with the 21 percent trend there would have been no savings. (Those with a discerning eye may also wonder why claims dollars are rounded to the nearest million while claims savings are calculated to the nearest penny.)

Epidemiology

Let's start with the epidemiology, which requires dividing the population into chronic and non-chronic, and using trend in the latter as a proxy for the former. This fails on two counts:

1. You can't divide a population into chronic versus non-chronic and expect people to stay put in their assigned cohort.
2. The per-patient costs of chronic versus non-chronic migrate differently. You can't use one as a proxy for the other.

So, basically—even before we get to the arithmetic—the whole concept of dividing the population into two defined cohorts falls flat on its face.

The first failure is the fact that people don't stay put: A substantial number of people not identified in the baseline with chronic disease have chronic disease events in the study year.[1] By condition, the percentages are as follows:

TABLE 1.2   Case-Mix of Members Hospitalized in 2005 by Chronic Condition

Category (members)	CAD	Asthma	CHF	Diabetes	Mean
(1) Admitted 2004 year and 2005	5.0%	4.9%	8.8%	11.0%	6.4%
(2) Not Admitted in 2004 and admitted in 2005	69.2%	55.7%	60.8%	36.7%	62.4%
(3) Members *undetected* in 2004 and admitted in 2005	9.0%	14.6%	8.7%	12.7%	10.0%
(4) New Members in 2005 and admitted in 2005	16.8%	24.8%	21.7%	39.6%	21.2%

Categories 3 and 4 represent 31 percent of the population. So the arithmetic assumption that a population can be *a priori* divided into non-disease and disease categories is not just a little wrong, but rather is substantially wrong.

Next, the consensus method claims "stability"[2] between the costs of the chronic and non-chronic populations over time. The correct interpretation, reflecting actual cost trends from 1997 to 2011, is that chronic disease costs in percentage terms rise more slowly than costs in the non-chronic population. This is easy for me to say—I've been writing requests for proposals (RFPs) longer than anyone by far. All I need to do is look at some old RFPs to see that, for example, average annual expense for a heart failure patient in 1998 was about $20,000 at a time when a person without chronic disease cost a health plan roughly $1,600/year—a multiple of 12.5 times. Today, heart failure patients average about $30,000/year while a member of a health plan without one of the five common chronic conditions costs more like $3,200—a multiple of 9.4 times. Though not a huge gap in absolute terms, a difference of this size matters a lot when claimed savings percentages are in the low single digits, like the example in the sidebar above.

I am not the only person to observe this divergence. Another study[3] looked at 16 combinations of four key variables to see whether these trends were similar or not. Those four variables were length of baseline, eligibility period, claims runout, and algorithm used to trigger identification as having the condition. Each of the four variables had two possibilities. Claims runout, for example, could be three months or six months. If you are keeping score at home and still smarting from being fooled into thinking "5 through 8" represented three chapters, this time we promise no funny business in the following arithmetic: Four variables with two possibilities per variable yield a total of 16 combinations of variables. One of the 16 comparisons showed similar chronic and non-chronic trends. Is the conclusion that there is only one way to design chronic and non-chronic trends to have the latter serve as a proxy for the former? Or should the conclusion be that if one tortures the data long enough it will confess?

The study author's guess is, quite correctly, the latter, because the particular combination of variables that resulted in similar chronic and non-chronic trends had no real theoretical justification other than being one of 16 that he tried. But as a practical matter, even though this author did identify one winning configuration of variables, it makes no difference because I've never once seen an outcomes report with a trend assumption based on that particular configuration.

The drawback of a study involving observations like these two epidemiological studies is that someone can (in the second case) "observe" the other conclusion to suit their bias, or (in the first case) concoct some data to the contrary to suit their bias. As Upton Sinclair said: "It is impossible to prove something to someone whose salary depends on believing the opposite." Or maybe it was Sinclair Lewis. I always get those two mixed up. Like you don't.

Math

So, the first point—the epidemiological one—can be argued. Pathetically, perhaps, but argued nonetheless. Let's then proceed to the second argument, the mathematical one. Fortunately, as we've described, math is not a "he said-she said" discipline. Math is proof-based. In the immortal words of the great philosopher Daniel P. Moynihan: "Everyone is entitled to their own opinions, but not to their own facts." Something is proven—a fact—if there are no possible exceptions to it, as with the Fermat's Last Theorem example presented earlier. Finding one exception to a proof invalidates it. In the case of the non-chronic-trend-as-proxy-for-trend canard, just like with the pre-post methodology generally, finding an exception doesn't even require breaking a sweat.

Once again, return to the two-asthmatic model. The population is divided at baseline into the disease population and the non-disease population. This division places Asthmatic #2 squarely within the non-disease population during the baseline period because no one at the health plan knows s/he has asthma since no claims have been incurred.* Asthmatic #2 is used as the "what-would-have-been" non-chronic trend for Asthmatic #1.

Person	2010 (baseline year)	2011 (contract year)
Asthmatic #1 —*Disease Population*	$2,000	$200
Asthmatic #2 —*Non-Disease Population*	$0	$2,000

Note that the $2,000 cost of an event does not rise between years, meaning that actual unit cost inflation is 0 percent. However, you would never guess that to be the case, if you used the non-chronic trend to estimate the chronic trend. You'd think healthcare inflation was out of control, rising in this admittedly extreme example by an infinite amount. The already-brilliant job of appearing to reduce spending on the disease population by 90 percent ($2,000 down to $200) becomes Nobel Prize-worthy in an environment of infinite healthcare inflation.

---

*Asthmatic #2 is identified as "healthy" for the purpose of trend calculation because s/he fits one or more of the nine categories listed on page 4 in the "Why Might a Member Not Be Identifiable" box.

Voilà. Using the mathematical axiom that an assertion is invalidated by one example to the contrary, the assertion that non-chronic trend can be used as a proxy for chronic trend is toast. Nonetheless, let's go a step further and create an example to see what happens over time.

In this next three-year table, some members categorized as healthy in the base year (2010) really do have asthma, and all those unidentified asthmatic members have the chance of having an asthma event. No, not every asthmatic's costs will look like #2 in the previous example, but enough do to inflate the non-chronic trend. *This happens because the year-over-year cost increase, up to and including the event, is counted in the what-would-have-been trend calculation.*

If all of us were implanted with transponders that immediately notified our health plan as soon as we crossed a line into having a chronic condition, the pre-post methodology would separate the two populations perfectly. Consider my favorite interviewer, Tim Russert. He was widely assumed during his lifetime to be a non-chronic person with no obvious health problems* and therefore would have been in the non-chronic cohort. His totally unanticipated heart attack therefore incorrectly inflates the non-chronic cohort trend when—with this magic transponder—his event should have been inflating the chronic disease trend.

Yes, we know that unlike most heart attack victims, he died at the scene and therefore incurred no claims expense. *Assuming he had survived*, his claims cost would have been counted in the non-chronic group. Please do us both a favor and try to focus on the bigger picture, okay? Thank you.

Generalizing from his case, absent that magical transponder, *it is inevitable that some chronically ill people will sneak into the non-chronic comparison group and thereby exaggerate the true cost trend of the non-chronic population when they have events.*

Return to the three-year example, and now add a row showing the impact on trend of chronic people being counted as non-chronic:

---

*Aside from having the world's third-widest head, behind (#2) Alec Baldwin and (#1) Stewey Griffin.

	2010 (Baseline)	2011 (Contract Year 1)	2012 (Contract Year 2)
Status	Not in program	Added to population going forward	In population
Asthmatic #2's costs	$0	$2,000	$200
Change attributed to the DM program using either methodology	*N/A*	*$0*	*−$1,800 (savings)*
Change in cost added to the what-would-have-been trend calculation from previous year		*+$2,000*	
Summary of Asthmatic #2's impact on trend (2010–2011) and savings (2011–2012)		***2010–2011 non-chronic trend is increased by $2,000***	***2011–2012 program savings is increased by $1,800***

The distortion in the disease population's costs over time is exacerbated by the calculation of trend in the non-disease population.

The way you can tell this is happening in reports presented to you is to see if there is a decline in every category of cost, including categories (like drugs and doctor visits) that should be rising in a preventive system. We'll show three examples of this in the case studies.

The reason you know a decline in all categories can't happen is, in reality and in accurately measured programs, claims in pharmacy and primary care always increase if a population health improvement program is successful, as more people substitute preventive drugs and physician care for hospitalizations and emergency room (ER) care. Our ongoing analogy: insulating your house reduces your energy expense, but your insulation expense rises.

A decline in cost across all claims categories versus trend can be due only to an overstatement of trend, which in turn is a result of putting chronically ill but undiagnosed people in the non-chronic-disease category.

Some of you might be wondering whether the effect of chronic members accidentally assigned to the non-chronic group is offset by the reverse happening, meaning non-chronic members accidentally assigned to the chronically ill group. The answer is, no. In fact, once again, mathematically this mis-assignment would exacerbate the difference in trend between the two groups. It's much rarer for someone to be thought to have (for example) heart disease and not actually have it than the reverse. Hence this next example is a rather unlikely one, but we shall soldier on with it even so. Suppose someone was misdiagnosed with a heart attack in the baseline year, and therefore the $20,000 cost of that person's *faux* heart attack was added into the baseline. Since the person didn't really have heart disease, his costs—which affect the cost of the chronic disease cohort as a group—will likely fall quite precipitously in the following year.

Why does all this happen? How can a well-intentioned committee building a consensus methodology—as well as most of the case studies we will be citing—be so far off? The arithmetic underlying their mistake is quite simple: When they calculate the average costs for a group of individuals with a disease, they don't count individuals with zero costs for that disease* in their average baseline. This causes the average baseline to be overstated, as shown in the first annual requalification example.

Consider a calculation of the average altitude of all the airplanes in the country. By averaging the radar readings, we learn that the average altitude of all the flights in the air (the ones the radar can spot) is 20,000 feet at a point in time. However, the radar has no way of finding planes on the ground. If half the planes in the country are

---

*In the case of Medicaid, those are often people who are eligible for coverage but who have not enrolled because they have no healthcare costs.

on the ground at any given time, then the average altitude of all the planes is 10,000 feet once the half on the ground is averaged with the half in the air.

A claims extraction algorithm is like that radar, averaging the claims only for people who have enough claims to be noticed, but excluding people who are, in terms of their claims, like the planes on the ground. Excluding individuals with no costs from an average will cause the calculated average to inflate the actual average. Yet, like the planes on the ground, the zero-cost patients—the patients in the "Why a Patient Might Not Be Visible" box—can't be counted because they can't be found.

Recall that the annual requalification method finds no change in the cost per asthmatic.

Person	2010	2011
Asthmatic #1	$2,000	$0
Asthmatic #2	$0 (invisible)	$2,000
Cost/Asthmatic using Prospective Identification	*$2,000*	*$1,000*
Cost/Asthmatic using Annual Requalification	*$2,000*	*$2,000*

If everybody had that aforementioned magical transponder implanted inside them that beamed a signal to the health plan or vendor the minute their physiology changed from healthy to unhealthy, there would be no invisible asthmatics, no "planes on the ground," ever. In that case, Asthmatic #2 would be counted as an asthmatic in 2010 and Asthmatic #1 would be counted in 2011, yielding the following analysis, which is, of course, the true cost:

Person	2010	2011
Asthmatic #1	$2,000	$0
Asthmatic #2	$0	$2,000
True Cost/Asthmatic	*$1,000*	*$1,000*

Likewise, in the other example in which Asthmatic #1 incurred $200 in claims in 2011, counting Asthmatic #2 in 2010 reveals that claims rose 10 percent.

Person	2010	2011
Asthmatic #1	$2,000	$200
Asthmatic #2	$0	$2,000
Cost/Asthmatic using Annual Requalification	*$2,000*	*$1,100*
True Cost/Asthmatic	*$1,000*	*$1,100*

Therefore, the two basic tenets on which the entire population health improvement industry is built, pre-post measurement and trending using the non-chronics, are both provably wrong, as a matter of both epidemiology and math. Still, in the interest of fairness, we should let the consulting/vendor industry counter this proof with a counterproof.

The Industry Counterproof to the Epidemiology and the Math

Gotcha! The *counterproof* turns out to be a trick question for two reasons. First, it isn't a question. Second, in math, there is no such thing as a counterproof, which is why if you google the word *counterproof* you get mostly references to engraving. Also, apparently there is a rock group by that name.*

In math, once something is proven, the case is closed because proving the opposite—that is, the aforementioned counterproof—would be impossible. Unfortunately, one of the themes in this book is that many people in the health management industry are unfamiliar with the concept of mathematical impossibility. As John Kenneth Galbraith said, "Faced with a proof that their belief is wrong, 10 percent will accept the proof while the other 90 percent will immediately get to work defending their belief."

---

*Yes, we agree. That's a dumb name for a rock group. However, rock historians have concluded that most of the good names were used up by about 1985 (along with most of the good songs).

If there were such a thing as a counterproof, defenders of the industry guidelines would claim that they do "adjust" for regression to the mean (all the objections we've been talking about, except the trend issue, fall into the category of regression to the mean). They do so by adding a "lookback" year prior to the baseline, a year in which people who happened to have zero disease-identifiable costs, or be "planes on the ground" during the baseline year itself might have had claims to identify them as having the condition in question. Unfortunately, if you review the list of reasons people with a condition might not be identified in the baseline year, you will see that few people excluded for any of those reasons would be found using a lookback year. To be found through a lookback year but not found in the baseline year, you'd have to have been in the health plan for at least two years *and* have been sick enough to qualify two years ago but not a year ago.

This isn't the only adjustment. The CCA Outcomes Guidelines, following explicit recognition of the limitations of conventional pre-post methodologies, contain page after page of adjustments and alternative methodologies and other caveats to their various methodologies, none of which change the basic problem, which is that the standard methodology is invalid. You can adjust Creationism all you want but it won't result in evolution.

They'd also say that my two-asthmatic example is an extreme one, which of course it is, for the purposes of illustration. Plug any less extreme numbers into those examples, and you'll still get a wrong answer. Not as far off, but wrong nonetheless. That real-life "What a Difference a Trend Makes" sidebar shows that you don't have to be far off—a few percentage points either way totally distorts the underlying result.

That's the epidemiologic problem with their rebuttal. The arithmetic problem with that rebuttal is simple: *An invalid equation cannot be made more valid by adding more numbers to it*. This is amply demonstrated by the immortal words of the great philosopher Captain Louis Renault: "Owing to the seriousness of this crime, I've instructed my men to round up twice the usual number of suspects."

To test that statement (meaning mine), simply go back to all the little asthma tables and substitute a multi-year baseline for a one-year baseline. Call the baseline however many years you want. Instead of "2010," call it "2006 to 2010." You'll notice that adding years does not create a valid outcome.

What have we learned so far, less than one chapter into *Why Nobody Believes the Numbers*? Quite a bit, it would appear:

1. Like delivering soliloquies, proposing marriage, and cooking broth, math should not be conducted by committee.
2. Trend is invariably going to be measured wrong in pre-post population-based studies—invariably in the direction of overstating the savings in the chronic disease population.
3. There is nothing at all in the realm of either epidemiology or (especially) arithmetic that should lead anyone to use non-chronic trend to predict chronic trend—and yet people do.

Fortunately, there is a way to make lemonade out of the consensus pre-post lemon and turn that methodology into something that mathematicians might recognize as provably valid, and we'll do that next. Epidemiologists and health services researchers will have to wait until Chapter 2 to have their concerns addressed. For now, the solution is to fix the problems in the consensus methodology to create a valid pre-post equation.

Fixing the Problem...at Least in Theory

Earlier we noted that the conventional pre-post method would be valid if transponders were implanted in us because then we would know in 2010 who had the disease in 2010, and could put those people in the baseline, whether or not they had claims.

But what if we used a proxy measure? Instead of qualifying people annually, or prospectively, what if we qualified them *retrospectively*, so that once a member shows up as having (for example) asthma in the contract year, we retrospectively include their "zeroes" to recalculate the baseline average claims per member? Ultimately—and it might take a couple of years—all the people who had asthma, diagnosed or not, in 2010 would be populated in the official 2010 asthma baseline.

Start with what is believed at the end of 2010 about the asthma population—there is one asthmatic who cost $2,000:

Person	2010
Asthmatic #1	$2,000
Cost/Asthmatic	*$2,000*

The existence of the second asthmatic becomes evident a year later. Populating that asthmatic in the table not just in 2011 (when he is known about) but also in 2010 (when he also had asthma but hadn't been considerate enough to bother telling anyone at the health plan) is exactly what is shown in the last table from the previous section: a valid reflection of actual cost of both asthmatics over both years.

Person	2010 (re-calculated following 2011)
Asthmatic #1	$2,000
Asthmatic #2	$0
Cost/Asthmatic	*$1,000*

This valid methodology is called "retrospective identification," as distinguished from the prospective identification and annual requalification methodologies. Here is the table as it looks following 2011, with both asthmatics counted in both years:

Person	2010	2011
Asthmatic #1	$2,000	$200
Asthmatic #2	$0	$2,000
Cost/Asthmatic using Retrospective Identification	*$1,000*	*$1,100*

It turns out that whereas other methodologies yield correct answers on any given data set about as often as Jupiter aligns with Mars when the moon is in the Seventh House, the retrospective methodology yields correct answers on every given data set. No exceptions. Naturally, being the only mathematically valid population-based methodology in an industry notorious for invalidity, it will come as no surprise that no one currently uses it.

It might also come as a surprise there are two shockingly good reasons not to use it. First, recalculating the baseline every year adds more complexity and uncertainty to a process that for most people is already neither simple nor certain. Second, there is a danger we may *over*-count people with disease. The epidemiology of adding Asthmatic #2's 2010 claims to the baseline once he is revealed as an asthmatic in 2011 is probably sound. He probably did have asthma in 2010. But continually adding people to the baseline once they present with a sentinel event in an "out" year, and then recalculating the baseline to include their claims during that year would be valid only if indeed everyone revealing themselves with a chronic disease in any contract year actually did have the disease in the baseline year. As the contract years accumulate, this approach would overcount people with the disease back in the baseline, adding too many people who really didn't have the condition several years prior to their presentation with it.

The math works every time, but the epidemiology doesn't. It is important nonetheless to show that the math works, to wrap up the discussion of methodologies where the math *doesn't* work to prove that non-working math need not be an integral component of outcomes methodologies. Also, now we have a sound methodology, a methodology that—if we could approximate it in the real world under real-world constraints—would be a useful and reasonably valid tool.

That's precisely where we are going from here: The remainder of this chapter shows how to modify the consensus pre-post formula to approximate the underlying mathematically valid retrospective methodology while still being epidemiologically cogent. Then—because these modifications are observational and not strictly mathematical—the next chapter will show how to test the result via observation, using "plausibility indicators," to satisfy your inner epidemiologist.

$10,000 Reward to Anyone Who Can Prove the Retrospective Methodology Invalid

The author is offering a $10,000 reward to the first industry trade or professional association, outcomes committee, benefits consulting firm, actuarial firm, U.S. citizen, or undocumented alien with a fake Social Security card who proves that, for population-based pre-post analysis, this retrospective qualification methodology is mathematically invalid and that their methodology is valid. Details of the contest are on the www.dismgmt.com website.

Approximating the Valid Methodology in Practice: The Dummy Year Adjustment

Creating a measure that avoids the over/under-counting dilemma requires the use of probabilities. For example, we can't say with more than 25 percent certainty that *exactly* two of four coin flips will be "heads". However, we can say with close to 100 percent certainty that *roughly* 2,000 of 4,000 coin flips will be "heads". Returning to the two-asthmatic illustration helps show how we might apply probabilities to address measuring wellness or disease management efficacy.

Person	2010	2011
Asthmatic #1	$2,000	$200
Asthmatic #2	$0	$2,000
Cost/Asthmatic using either prospective identification or annual requalification	*$2,000*	*$1,100*

In the absence of any intervention at all, the pre-post methodology generates a whopping 45 percent cost decline. But suppose performing this year-over-year comparison using several different year-pairings—observing what happens in 2010 versus 2009 and 2009 versus 2008—consistently yields a decline similar to 45 percent.

It then becomes possible to compensate for the savings overstated by the invalid pre-post metrics: The first 45 percent of decline would be attributable to the methodology's inherent invalidity, while any further decline would be attributable to the program. The difference between these hypothetical pre-program year-over-year results and subsequent year results could then be used to create an adjustment factor to distinguish program effects from automatic methodology effects.

This factor is called a "Dummy Year Adjustment," and the act of applying it is called a "Dummy Year Analysis." Conveniently, both can be abbreviated as DYA. To return to the coin flip metaphor, consider a situation in which all asthmatics with high enough costs to be identified are "heads" in the baseline year, and 60 percent flip over to "tails" (meaning they become too low-cost to be identified) in the contract year. A typical contractual methodology would credit the vendor with the full 60 percent reduction, but this DYA-based calculation would recognize that 50 percent of heads would flip to "tails" on their own, and credit the vendor only with the additional 10 percent.

DYAs are generated by looking across multiple year-pairings. However, expense, time, or unavailability of data may limit the DYA calculation to two or three year-pairs. One typical *modus operandi* is to analyze two dummy year pairings, and if the calculated year-over-year decline is similar in each one, the average of the two declines becomes the DYA. If the year-pairing declines are dissimilar, a third and even fourth year-pairing is undertaken in order to hone in on the decline due to methodology.

Wait a Second—Aren't Those Different People in Each Year-Pairing?

Of course. In DM you're always talking about different people in each year. But it's the same condition, the same algorithm, the same organization. Especially if you run multiple dummy year-pairings, the people involved in each year-pairing should have similar characteristics as a whole, even if they are not the same exact people.

It is hard to imagine the Illinois state government producing a "Gallant" example of anything involving moral or financial integrity, being a "Goofus"* type of state in those two respects.** Nonetheless, an excellent real-world example of a DYA would be Illinois Medicaid's "frequent flyer" emergency room diversion program.

The state's Medicaid agency wanted to identify and educate high ER utilizers about using alternatives to the ER, and then measure to see if that education made a difference in their subsequent ER utilization. Instead of just identifying everyone who had five or more visits in a year, educating them, and seeing how many visits they made the subsequent year, they started by tracking the subsequent year's performance for high utilizers *before* a program was put in place. It turned out that as a group, people with five or more visits in a single year went to the ER 40 percent less in the subsequent year even without a program, meaning that one year's highest ER utilizers were not necessarily the next year's highest utilizers. This regression-to-the-mean decline proved remarkably consistent over five retrospective year-pairings.

So instead of crediting the vendor with gross reductions in utilization of the ER by the identified high utilizers in the baseline, the state credited the vendor only with reductions beyond the automatic 40 percent heads-to-tails effect. This resulted in the vendor showing modest improvements rather than the massive savings they would have taken the credit for otherwise.

Postscript: Illinois can't stay out of character for long and will make a cameo in the "100% Club" later on in this book, enthusiastically joining the list of states claiming more savings than the amount they spend on chronic disease events, thus violating the rule in math that you can't reduce a number by more than 100 percent no matter how hard you try. And rules in math are so strictly enforced that even Rod Blagojevich can't violate them.

---

*Gallant politely reminds readers that both he and Goofus are registered trademarks of *Highlights for Children*. Goofus sprinkles Gallant's DNA at a crime scene.

**Statistically speaking, you have a better chance of going to jail in Illinois by becoming governor than if you kill someone.

SOME DO'S AND DON'TS FOR DUMMY YEAR ADJUSTMENTS

The DYA fixes the annual requalification methodology by canceling out its invalidity. (Prospective identification is too invalid to be fixed by anything.) However, a methodology has to be applied consistently year over year in order for the DYA to yield similar results in each year-pairing. A year with a lot of outliers—a year in which a significant benefits design change took place, or a year with a significant demographic change—will skew the results on either end of the year-pairing. And for that matter, it would skew other methodologies even more than they are already skewed.

For instance, a dramatic reduction in co-pays for preventive drugs or a dramatic increase in co-pays for ER visits might be enough of a change to bend the event rates with or without a care management program. Likewise, although steady aging in a population will not affect the DYA calculation, a layoff, early retirement incentive, or merger will prevent a consistent result. These confounding variables make it impossible to attribute or even correlate an outcome with a program no matter what methodology is used.

Confounding variables do not necessarily undermine the usefulness of the DYA. The benefits design change has to be a substantial one in order to throw off the calculation, since any design change would have to strongly discourage or encourage preventive or curative care relative to the previous year. Finally, the "plausibility test" discussed later will be able to approximate the impact of these confounding variables.

As with any methodology and not surprisingly quite the contrary to most other guidelines, it is preferable to use the DYA on units of utilization, rather than on unit costs. Adding unit costs into the equation adds the likelihood of mistakes due to variations in inflation trend. As noted earlier, using the non-chronic trend to estimate chronic trend will usually, if not always, overstate actual inflation. And as noted in the example sidebar, the magnitude of the trend adjustment tends to overwhelm the magnitude of the savings.

The problem in using dollars for a DYA is that actual inflation itself, even if validly calculated, also varies by year. Also, because unit cost contracting is not involved in any care management initiative, the likelihood that using cost-based metrics will add any insight is overwhelmed by the likelihood of distortion. The focus of disease management is on reducing units of care, not the contracted cost per unit of care. Hence, there is no analytical reason to try to factor the latter into the calculation.

The DYA factor is accurate only if the previous program (the one in place during the year-pairings) was ineffective or nonexistent. In those cases, the entire year-over-year reduction would be due to the methodology. The DYA loses its usefulness when the program in place during the dummy year-pairings was equally effective during all the years in the pairings, meaning that program effectiveness could be a confounding variable for the methodology overstatement in the year-pairings. Suppose, for example, that a DYA consistently shows, for example, a 5 percent savings in different year-pairings. How can we know much (if any) of that 5 percent is due to the previous program rather than the methodology?

The next chapter answers that question using an observational analysis based on event rate measurement called a "plausibility test." In almost any population health improvement program, the savings can only come from reducing adverse events (or some other easily trackable resource, like specialist visits). If the plausibility test reveals no changes in adverse event rates, then the year-over-year reductions shown by a pre-post—even with a DYA—will be due to regression to the mean. If, however, the plausibility test shows that an organization has enjoyed a reduction in event rates from previous years, the year-over-year cost improvement was due at least in part to event avoidance. ·

Let's close this chapter with one takeaway that binds the math together, a takeaway that is quite the opposite of most other guidelines, and one that can be applied generally to life. We, too, will use bold italics, accepting the risk that the CCA may sue us for font infringement:

> ***Test multiple methodologies on a simple hypothetical where the right answer is obvious to the naked eye. The methodology that yields that naked-eye answer is the right methodology. All further refinements should be applied to that methodology (or an approximation of that methodology), as no amount of refining can turn invalid methodologies into valid ones.***

Chapter 2

**Plausibility Testing:
How to Measure Outcomes
Using Ingredients You Already
Have in Your Kitchen**

As stated succinctly by the immortal philosopher Humpty Dumpty, "When I use a word, it means just what I choose it to mean, neither more nor less." In outcomes measurement, that's the case with plausibility testing. Since I am the first person to apply this term to this field, I can choose it to mean whatever I want. And I define it as "using screamingly obvious techniques to check whether a claimed statement is valid, techniques that despite their validity your vendors and consultants will nonetheless discourage you from applying, for reasons of their own."

This second half of this definition is unique to health management, but no one is a stranger to the first half. In everyday life, you apply "screamingly obvious techniques to check whether a claimed statement is valid" so instinctively that you don't even realize you are applying a plausibility test. For instance, suppose you, your spouse, and your daughter Jennifer are enjoying a family dinner one night and Jennifer's cell phone rings. She excuses herself, goes in the other room for a few minutes, comes back out and announces, "Mom, Dad, I'm going over to Jason's house tonight to do homework."

No doubt you reply, "Okay, bye. Have a nice time." Ha ha, good one, Al. Obviously you don't say that. You say: "Wait a second. Who's Jason? What subject? Are his parents home?" Then you call over to the house to make sure that (1) adults answer the phone and that (2) the particular adults who answer the phone do indeed have a son named Jason.

You are testing the *plausibility* of Jennifer's statement, so instinctively, so reflexively, that you don't even think, let alone, say: "Honey, I think we have to test the plausibility of this story."

That's everyday life. For some reason—and we will offer some theories—when it comes to care management program outcomes, people suspend their disbelief rather than check plausibility. They often accept sky-high savings estimates, often mathematically impossible ones, as we will see in myriad examples, rather than plausibility-test them.

Plausibility testing has two different applications:

1. The narrower—the one used when someone asks: "Did you plausibility-test this result?"—is to see if the claimed savings could have been achieved in a disease management program by adverse medical event reduction, or in other program types, by analogous categories of savings or risk reduction to be discussed later.

2. The broader application is the *Seven Rules of Plausibility*—the check-off list that every outcomes report must satisfy. We'll list these rules in the next chapter, give brief examples of each, and then, to keep your attention from flagging, quote yet another immortal philosopher, this time Ned Flanders. Then we will dissect some case studies of violating them.

To start with, here is a brief vignette of the application of a plausibility test. Suppose you are presented a 10 percent claimed reduction in overall expense through chronic disease management. ER visits and hospitalizations comprise roughly half of total costs (see Appendix for typical percentages of costs in each major resource category) and are by far the major, if not the only, savings opportunity in straight disease management. Therefore, they would have to fall by 20 percent to achieve that 10 percent overall savings.

Next, figure only half of all hospitalizations/ER visits are avoidable through population-based programs. (The Appendix suggests that this estimate is generous. Also, the Agency for Health Quality and Research puts out a consensus list of avoidable hospitalizations through better ambulatory care, covering much less than a quarter of all hospitalizations, so "about half" is a generous assumption.) You would then need to see a 40 percent reduction in avoidable hospitalizations to generate a 10 percent net savings. So, you check your rate of avoidable hospitalizations to see if it fell by 40 percent. It's a simple observation. The savings have to come from utilization reduction *somewhere*, right? By definition, only an idiot wouldn't try to confirm the existence of savings by seeing if savings exist, right?

Wrong.

Consultants, vendors, and, yes, the CCA guidelines *discourage* doing a plausibility test, the word appearing only three times in that particular document. (The earlier editions contained much more information about doing the test.)

A cynic might say that attitude by itself is an excellent reason to undertake such a simple and obvious test. A cynic might also say that benefits consultants oppose plausibility testing because it is too easy, and doesn't require retaining their services, and that vendors oppose plausibility testing because they fear that Toto might pull the curtain away from their fancy metrics. Basically, using the cynical view, a lot of people would lose a lot of money if plausibility testing replaced pre-post.

Cynics may also direct their cynicism at me and say: "Maybe there is something wrong with a plausibility test, if no one else uses it other than Al." *Au contraire*, as I mentioned earlier, about 40 health plans, employers, and states (Ohio, Utah, and Wyoming) use it. True, those 40 payers represent only about 5 percent of patients, but what I didn't mention earlier is that they've won about 90 percent of the major national awards for valid outcomes.*

---

*The most respected national award is the list of "best payors in disease management," in the *Annual Report on the Disease Management and Wellness Industries,* now published by the Institute for Health and Productivity Management. Ohio, Utah, Wyoming, Procter & Gamble, and others—almost all of which plausibility-test their results—are recognized for program quality.

Plausibility Testing: The Event Rate Test Explained

To paraphrase the immortal words of the great philosopher Frank Morgan, pay no attention to that man behind the keyboard. Don't take my word for the value of plausibility testing or anything else in this or any other math book. See for yourself. You've already seen how pre-post analysis works. Now, do the same for plausibility testing. Here is how a plausibility test works, for asthma:

> **A.** Count how many asthma attacks requiring ER and inpatient care you incurred in the baseline years, and any underlying utilization trend in prior years suggesting that number might rise or fall on its own. (Usually, for asthma in a commercial population without disease management, the number of attacks stays roughly flat.)
>
> **B.** Count how many asthma attacks you had in the study year.
>
> **C.** The difference is the number of attacks you avoided.

A minus *B* equals *C*. Savings may be estimated by incorporating the cost of an attack (ER and inpatient) into the calculation, and then subtracting the costs of the extra preventive drug therapy and the DM program. ("Whole person" management involves avoiding and measuring co-morbidities too. This is discussed in the sidebar below.)

Phrased that way, the rationale for event rate observation is straightforward. Disease management saves payors money and improves member health by avoiding adverse medical events— inpatient stays and ER visits—in the categories most closely associated with the condition *across the entire population*. So, for instance, an asthma DM program should reduce the number of asthma attacks. A wellness program would reduce risk factors and adverse events caused by risk factors. Carrying the plausibility logic further, patient-centered medical homes (PCMH) should reduce four things:

> **1.** Adverse events, due to better care.
>
> **2.** Total ER visits, due to expanded primary care access.
>
> **3.** Specialist visits, due to emphasis on getting care from one's primary physician.

4. High-cost diagnostic tests, which are often re-administered in a fragmented system but which are supposed to be coordinated in a PCMH model, thanks to the electronic health record.

We will check on PCMH success at achieving most of those reductions later in the book. For the time being, suffice it to say it's a bit premature to invest your 401K in PCMH stocks.

Wait a Second. I Thought We Were Supposed to "Manage the Whole Patient" in Disease Management. Aren't You Saying the Exact Opposite?

Not at all. You are simply testing the plausibility of your alleged whole-patient results when you look at the reduction in disease-specific events. If you are managing the whole patient, your total savings, including co-morbidities, should be multiples of the savings from avoiding events in the disease itself. The size of the "comorbidity multiplier" depends on the condition. Asthmatics are generally pretty healthy if asthma is their biggest issue, and hence have essentially no other areas for improvement, whereas people with heart failure are quite ill and have many more manageable comorbidities that ebb and flow with their overall health. Typical comorbidity multipliers are as follows:

Asthma	1x (no savings potential through comorbid event reduction)
Ischemic cardiac disease	1.5x
CHF	3x
COPD	2x
Diabetes	3x

So, if you can identify, for example, 100 avoided diabetes-specific events, by managing the "whole diabetes patient" you probably avoided 300 events overall in the diabetes population.

One way to validate program success, then, is to monitor the rate of relevant medical events (and, for PCMH, resource uses) in the population. If the rate of relevant events in a population declines, assuming no significant change in the rate nationally and no significant change in the plan demographics,* the intervention was certainly correlated with and probably caused a positive effect. If not, it didn't.

You might say, "So, in other words, you see how many disease-related adverse events you had in the baseline versus how many you have now and credit the program with the difference. Doesn't the pre-post methodology do exactly the same thing? How else can you know how many events you avoided, other than by counting them? Doesn't everybody do this?"

Alas, no, everybody does not do this. As mentioned, plausibility testing is too easy to require consultants, and runs the risk of showing no reduction, which could be costly for vendors.

As a result, for years many organizations have been managing (for example) cardiac disease in order to prevent heart attacks, without ever noting whether their heart attack rate is higher or lower than average, or whether it is declining faster or slower than average. Indeed, few health plan executives, and almost no human resource administrators or their consultants, even know what their organization's heart attack rate is. Do you know what your organization's is? I didn't think so.

Pre-post methodology emphatically does *not* count events, and certainly does not compare events to an average or see whether they are declining. The key to event rate analysis—what makes it different from pre-post analysis, in which only the pre-identified "heads" have their subsequent events counted in the contract year—*is to count every event every year*. Using an extreme example illustrates both the flaw in the traditional pre-post approach and the difference between pre-post and plausibility. A birth rate is the number of

---

*I am often asked: "What about turnover? Doesn't high turnover distort the metrics?" Answer: It makes the vendor's job much harder, since people they've been working with leave and new people come in, but if turnover doesn't change the age/sex makeup of the population, the metrics still work. The results will be disappointing, but the metrics work.

babies delivered during the year divided by the total number of members. There are two ways you can measure that year over year:

1. Defining the potential pool for calculating a subsequent year's birthrate as a pre-selected "baseline" group of females deemed likely to have babies based on their claims history (pre-post).
2. Dividing the number of babies born by the total population every year (plausibility).

To illustrate the difference in the approaches, assume in the hypothetical below that first-time moms account for 25 percent of all babies.

	Births Using the Event Rate "Plausibility Test"	Births Using Pre-Post Analysis
Pool	Everyone (*e.g.*, 100,000)	All mothers identified through claims data to have had babies last year (1,000). This is the "potential mother cohort."
Baseline Number of Babies (the number born last year)	1,000	1,000
Contract Year Number of Babies Counted	1,000	750 (1,000 babies less the 250 born to moms who weren't in the mother cohort the previous year)
Actual Number of Babies in Contract year	1,000	1,000
Difference between Actual and Counted	0	250

Plausibility 1, Pre-post 0.

Another way to look at event rate measurement compared to pre-post analysis is to return once again to the example of the two-person asthma population:

Person	2010	2011
Asthmatic #1	$2,000	$0
Asthmatic #2	$0	$2,000
Event Rate Plausibility Analysis—Number of Attacks Observed	*1*	*1*
Pre-Post Analysis Number of Attacks (counted only in the pre-identified population)	*0*	*1*

The event rate-driven plausibility test provides a valid figure by counting both the asthma attack for Asthmatic #1 in 2010 and the asthma attack for Asthmatic #2 in 2011. The pre-post does not count events accurately because Asthmatic #2 does not show up in the pool whose events are tallied in 2011. Just as counting births is the easiest and most valid way to measure changes in the birth are, counting adverse medical events is the easiest and most valid way to measure changes in the adverse event rate. A self-evident statement? Indeed, and yet one honored mostly in the breach by consultants and vendors, because it costs them money.

That is why consultants and vendors generally don't support plausibility tests, and why we recommend plausibility tests. After you've run this simple plausibility test using data that you have easy access to, you then know that the claimed 45 percent reduction using pre-post can't possibly be accurate.

Plausibility 2, Pre-post 0.

EXAMPLES OF EVENT RATE-BASED PLAUSIBILITY TESTS

Massachusetts is home to the top-rated health plan in the country (as well as the top-rated Blue Cross plan, that more than coincidentally also excels at disease management, and—while we are on the subject of boasting about my home state—excellent clam chowder, some generally competent sports teams, and politicians who can hold a

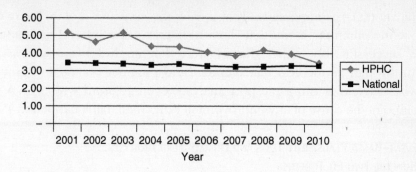

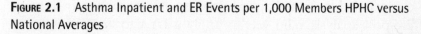

FIGURE 2.1 Asthma Inpatient and ER Events per 1,000 Members HPHC versus National Averages

debate without the "highlights" being posted to YouTube). Figure 2.1 is an example of an asthma event rate analysis from Harvard Pilgrim, the aforementioned Massachusetts health plan ranked #1 in the country by the National Committee for Quality Assurance since 2003, and one of America's two or three most successful health plans at event rate reduction. The chart shows the decline in the combination of asthma-related emergency room visits and inpatient admissions per 1,000 members.

Note that the asthma rate is compiled per 1,000 commercial members, not per 1,000 asthmatics. No one can be sure who the asthmatics are before they reveal themselves as asthmatics via claims, which can happen well after the "pre" population is determined in a pre-post calculation. Instead, this is a simple observation of asthma-related events.

The observed decline in Harvard Pilgrim's asthma events is meaningful only in the context of the national or regional rate of asthma events. This national rate (in this case) averages many health plans and large self-insured employers using the same algorithm to observe asthma attacks—a primary-coded 493.xx claim, with a place of service of the hospital or the ER. Conclusion after examining the surprisingly consistent, slightly declining, national asthma event rate: Harvard Pilgrim has improved its performance in asthma.

Even so, crediting the event rate improvement to the DM program—versus provider education or profiling, and/or other initiative(s)—is impossible. That is why the conclusion of an event-rate measurement is *not* that Harvard Pilgrim's specific DM program is successful, but rather that Harvard Pilgrim has been successful through its medical management and provider contracting as a whole. (Neither can a pre-post analysis, even adjusted with a DYA, pinpoint the cause of any improvement other than that it happened.)*

Event-Based Plausibility Tests and Dummy Year Analyses: How the Two Fit Together

We concluded the last chapter by saying that the only way to make a pre-post analysis valid was to apply a DYA to it. Then it seems like this chapter dismissed that whole idea and concludes by saying pre-post is a waste of time and you should use event rates instead. What gives?

A pre-post measurement using a DYA to neutralize its invalidity should yield a reasonably accurate dollar figure for savings. Dividing that gross savings figure by total claims spent on the conditions in question yields a gross savings percentage. Dividing that gross savings figure by program costs is how one calculates a return on investment, or ROI.

That should be a roughly correct ROI in theory thanks to the DYA. Even so, there are so many moving parts in a pre-post analysis that it is quite possible, to use a technical disease management term, to screw it up. Likewise, the signal-to-noise ratio is quite low in a pre-post, with or without a DYA, because so much cost moves in directions that have nothing to do with the intervention.

Applying a plausibility test—to make sure that the event rate trend inflection is consistent with the savings—confirms the pre-post if the percentage decline in events (adjusted for the change due to industry-wide care improvements, which will show up in the national average event rates) *at least* equals the claimed gross savings

---

*The prototypical example of a result that fails a plausibility test, to be discussed in Chapter 4, would be the aforementioned North Carolina Medicaid report of a 54 percent reduction in costs of neonates. The statewide database of neonatal discharges and days of care showed no utilization reduction, thus invalidating the Medicaid result.

percentage. "At least" because the gross savings percentage is an average of all costs impacted by disease management programs while the disease-specific event rates capture only a portion of potential savings—those associated with the events most likely to decline (adverse events in the condition being managed). It would be hard to imagine how an average of all cost categories could decline by, for example, 5 percent unless hospitalizations in the condition being managed—the only major cost category likely to decline at all in a DM program—decline by much more than that 5 percent.

If hospitalizations don't decline by much more than that 5 percent, it means the plausibility analysis fails to confirm the pre-post. In that case, you have two options:

1. Re-doing the pre-post to get it to conform to what we know is the case based on the plausibility indicators.
2. Asking yourselves, why bother with the costly and time-consuming pre-post when the plausibility analysis tells you what you need to know?

Some people will keep re-doing the pre-post to get it to match plausibility as opposed to the reverse, tacitly acknowledging that plausibility analyses are more valid than pre-post. So why keep torturing the pre-post data, at considerable effort and expense, to come up with a result if the plausibility test spells it right out? Maybe a pre-post analysis is specified by the vendor contract. Maybe the chief financial officer is insisting on a dollar-based ROI. Or maybe the benefits consultant has kids in college. But one way or another, plausibility analyses are often used just to confirm.

Plausibility tests are simple, valid, transparent, expeditious, almost mistake-proof* and inexpensive to perform. The biggest

---

*The most common "honest mistake" the vendor makes is to calculate the event rates on the pre-identified population, rather than the entire population. That calculation will always show declines because so many previously unidentified people have events. Like in car insurance, the pre-identified "high-risk pool" accounts disproportionately for accidents, but people with the "safe driver discount" get in accidents, too. That's why they have insurance.

objection to them in a non-confirming role is that they don't yield a dollar ROI. There is a way to calculate ROI, but it's too much detail for this book. In a nutshell, assign standard costs to each episode of inpatient and ER care (including post-event follow-up), and multiply that cost by the number of events you think you avoided. That will provide a bare minimum estimate of savings. "Bare minimum" because it doesn't include savings in events for related comorbidities, estimates of which were noted in the sidebar earlier in this chapter.

How to Actually Do a Plausibility Test

Enough chatter. In the old days when people made their own clothes, they'd haggle with the tradesperson for a while before actually buying the fabric. When they were ready to buy the fabric, they'd ask the tradesperson to tack it to the wall to measure it. The expression "Let's get down to brass tacks" derives from this practice (that's our story and we're sticking to it), and that's what we're about to do.

First, you start out by counting the number of ICD-9s, or someday hopefully in our natural lifetimes, ICD-10s, which will map to ICD-9s for historic comparisons. Table 2.1 is the chart, for each condition, that you might use.

You simply count the primary-coded events with a place-of-service of the ER or hospital, and add them up for each condition. Some people separate ER from inpatient. I don't. I focus on total

TABLE 2.1   ICD-9s by Chronic Condition

Chronic Condition	ICD-9 Codes (all xx unless otherwise indicated)
Asthma	493.xx (excluding 493.2x*)
Chronic Obstructive Pulmonary Disease	491.xx, 492.xx, 493.2x, 494.xx, 496.xx, 506.4x
Coronary Artery Disease (and related heart-health issues)	410, 411, 413, 414 (all .xx)
Diabetes (and common complications)	249.xx, 250.xx, 357.2, 681.1x, 682.6, 682.7, 785.4, 707, 731.8, 251.1, 251.2, 362.0, 366.41
Heart Failure	398.90. 398.91, 398.99, 402.01, 402.11, 402.91, 404.01, 404.03, 404.11, 404.13, 404.91, 404.93, 422.00, 422.9x, 425.xx, 428.xx, 429.xx, 674.5x

events. The ER/IP ratio can depend on other factors, like how many open beds there are in the hospital. Nonetheless, I do *look* at the ratios of ER/IP to see if they are in line with expectations. Otherwise, the data may have been collected wrong. For instance, ER visits may have been double-counted because the professional and facility claims were each tallied for the same event. Typical expectations of an ER/inpatient ratio might be:

Asthma	4:1
Chronic Obstructive Pulmonary Disease	1:1
Coronary Artery Disease	1:4
Congestive Heart Failure	1:6
Diabetes	1:1

Next, you count the number of people in your plan or employed population. If you are a health plan, you separate commercial members from Medicare members and do this analysis separately for each. Divide the number of PRIMARY-CODED events by the number of members to get an event rate. "Primary-coded" is capitalized to emphasize that you want to record the reason people went to the ER or hospital. It's also capitalized because when I present this material, I say "Count only the primary-coded ICD-9s" about eleventy gazillion times, give or take a few, but nonetheless invariably someone will ask me during the Q&A whether only the primary-coded ICD-9s should be counted.

Doing this analysis over multiple years is helpful because you can create a graph like the Harvard Pilgrim example above, or at least like the one shown in Figure 2.2. The one above requires a national comparison—more on that in a minute.

Figure 2.2 is a snapshot of an employer's primary-coded medical events per 1,000 covered lives over time, using data easily extractable from the data warehouse, at least in theory. What this analysis *doesn't* tell you is the answer to the age-old question posed by the immortal philosopher Henny Youngman: "'How's your wife?' 'Compared to what?'"

You can't know whether these trend lines are good, bad, or indifferent without determining a benchmark.

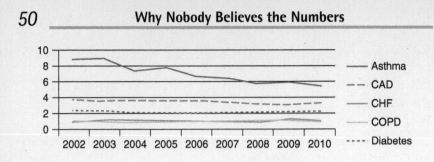

Figure 2.2   Harvard Pilgrim Event Rates 2002 to 2010

There are three ways to determine a benchmark. First, you could get your friends to use this exact same analysis on their populations, and compare that way, which is great if you (1) have friends who (2) are willing to do the analysis.

Second, you could go to the Agency for Healthcare Quality and Research's Healthcare Cost and Utilization Project website, http://hcupnet.ahrq.gov/HCUPnet.jsp. It's free and comprehensive. I use it all the time and tell everyone I meet about it with great enthusiasm. (Maybe that's why I never get invited to parties.) The drawbacks are that it is usually more than a year out of date (for instance, as of this writing in early 2012, 2010 was reported only for about 15 states) and it doesn't provide its event rates in per-1000 terms, so you have to use other census-based tools to translate the raw event numbers into a per-1,000 rate.

If all else fails, the worst-case scenario, which really isn't so terrible when you get right down to it, is to call me and have me do it for you. You get pretty clear output like the Harvard Pilgrim asthma example in the previous chapter and Figure 2.2. From those types of displays, you learn respectively how you are doing versus everyone else and versus your own history. You would learn that, in COPD, maintaining a constant event rate is a good thing while in CAD maintaining a constant event rate would lag the national average event rate trend, which is itself declining. Then, we turn it into an ROI using the standard-costing technique described above. The drawback of this approach is that it costs you money. Not much, but money nonetheless.

Here are the details that come up when you conduct a plausibility test on your own, in the form of answers to frequently asked questions minus the actual questions themselves:

1. Do not count the number of people (two discharges for one person equals one discharge for two people), and do not take into account whether people were in a disease management program.
2. Do not include people for whom you are secondary payer.
3. If someone has an event straddling the year-end, count that person in the year of discharge.
4. Add all the codes together in each disease category to create a total number of events.
5. Don't be concerned with taking out false positives; they will wash.
6. Use admissions, not bed-days.
7. If you are a Medicaid plan, do *not* use waivered populations. These indicators are specifically for TANF and adult blind and disabled. *No* aged. *All* primary-pay.
8. If someone is transferred between hospitals and has an applicable primary diagnosis both times, they count twice.
9. If someone has (for example) a heart attack and an angina attack in one hospitalization, only the primary discharge code counts.
10. Admissions following discharges count separately if they generate two different claims forms.
11. Interim submissions of claims or claims submissions replaced by other claims submissions should only be counted once (since they represent only one hospital stay).
12. Admissions made through the ER, of course, do not count as ER visits.

(continued)

(*continued*)

13. Claims may include facility and professional. Remember to only count facility and not professional claims—otherwise it is double-counting.

14. Urgent care is not the same as ER. Do not count urgent care. ER includes just (1) ER place of service and (2) observation days.

15. All hospital *and* **SNF** admissions count as inpatient, including <24 hours, and *excluding* observation days, which we count with ER.

16. Each event may have multiple bills, like the MD charge for the ER visit. Only count each event once.

17. Allowed claims, not paid claims (should be about the same thing).

18. Fiscal year or calendar year is fine—most people use calendar year.

19. Be careful that your case-finding algorithm notes that sometimes IP admissions from the ER take place the day after the ER admission (like at night).

20. Go back as many years as is conveniently trackable. The more years you go back, the more insight you will glean from the analysis.

21. Do *not* count members uniquely. Use an *average* member count—total member-months/12 or an average of members for the year, etc.

22. Do *every* one of the five conditions, even if you are not managing all of them. (The non-managed ones act as a kind of control.)

Chapter 3

Case Studies That Flunk Every Plausibility Test Known to Mankind

C hapters 3 and 4 of *Why Nobody Believes the Numbers* will be Case Studies in Cluelessness Gone Wild. First, some short vignettes and then, in Chapter 4, some more extensive and dramatic stories of the soon-to-be-a-major-motion-picture variety, starring Elizabeth Montgomery as the Outcomes Fairy. To totally understand what constitutes cluelessness and hence appreciate these case studies, you need to know the *Seven Rules of Plausibility*.

The Seven Rules of Plausibility

Everything in life has an "80–20" rule. Example: 20 percent of the population accounts for more than 80 percent of income; 80 percent of a ball club's salary goes to 20 percent of its players, and so forth. The 80–20 rule is everywhere.

In population health spending, the 80–20 rule is that 80 percent of the time, there is no 80–20 rule. For instance, the Centers for Disease Control claims that the 50 percent of adults who have chronic disease account for 75 percent of healthcare spending. A 75–50 rule is about as far from an 80–20 rule as you can get, and means that costs are diffused throughout the system, rather than concentrated. (It is also not the slightest bit clear how they can define "chronic disease" so broadly that fully 50 percent of us have it. Are they including insomnia? Tooth decay? Dandruff? Ring around the collar? And how do they even know I suffer from these afflictions, let alone how much I spend on white noise machines, toothpaste, or Head and Shoulders? Or whether I've discovered that Wisk around the collar beats ring around the collar? But we shall leave both these questions and Those Dirty Rings for another day.)

Consistent with that observation about unconcentrated costs, it turns out that large chunks of potential savings are not sitting in one place just waiting to be harvested by a vendor imploring people to smoke fewer Marlboros and eat more broccoli. Yes, the lesson from this chapter will be: A simple, usually voluntary, program isn't going to make a noticeable dent in health spending.

But try explaining this to the population health improvement industry, which prides itself on saying they do exactly that. Fortunately a modicum of math and critical thinking, using one or more of seven informal, common-sense rules can help determine whether this pride is justified. These rules are not footnoted or otherwise sourced, because there is no precedent and no governing body for validating PHI outcomes. Instead, you must make your own judgment as to whether common sense trumps vendor reporting.

Or, to quote the immortal words of the great philosopher Groucho Marx: "Who are you gonna believe, me or your own eyes?"

The goal of these common-sense rules is not to validate every study that is truly valid, which would be a Herculean task, but rather to invalidate those claims that are obviously invalid, a first level of intellectual triage to avoid making misguided resource allocation decisions. Even that seemingly modest level of intellectual triage will eliminate the majority of claimed results from consideration, allowing you to focus on evaluating interventions that might really work.

The plausibility rules are as follows, with their shorthand in boldface:

1. **The 100 Percent Rule**: Outcomes explicitly or implicitly cannot require any element of cost to decline by more than 100 percent.
2. **The Every Metric Can't Improve Rule**: Every element of resource use or group of people cannot decline in cost, through programs aimed generally at improving prevention. In

particular, the actual costs associated with prevention, such as primary care visits, drug use, and health screening, must rise.

3. **The 50 Percent Savings Rule**: In a voluntary health management program with no incentives, declines in excess of 50 percent in any given resource category are the result of invalidity, not effectiveness.

4. **The Nexus Rule**: There must be a logical link between the goal of the program and the source of savings.

5. **The Quality Dose–Cost Response Rule**: Just as in pharmacology, where there is an observable time-dependent relationship between dose and response, cost cannot decline significantly faster or more than the related quality variables improve.

6. **The Control Group Equivalency Rule**: Control groups, if not prospectively sorted into two similar or equivalent groups, based on objective data, before members are even contacted to determine willingness to enroll, are likely to mislead. This is especially true of *historic controls* (meaning pre-post), *matched controls*, and *using the non-disease group as a control for the disease group*.

7. **The Multiple Violations Rule**: When one of these rules is violated, others are likely to be violated, as well.

There is a concept in testing called "face validity," meaning what you'd expect it to mean: A study has face validity if it looks like it's fairly measuring what it's supposed to measure. These plausibility tests introduce a companion measure: "face impossibility." An example has face impossibility if rather than challenge the data or the study design to question an outcome, you can simply tell from the numbers themselves as presented by the vendor that the outcome is impossible. Every example in these two chapters has face impossibility.

THE *100 PERCENT* RULE: OUTCOMES CANNOT EXPLICITLY OR IMPLICITLY EXCEED 100 PERCENT

The textbook example of face impossibility is violating this plausibility rule: You cannot reduce a number by more than 100 percent, period. This is true no matter how hard you try. And just to avoid any potential misunderstandings by our readers Down Under, this also isn't one of those things that's the opposite in the Southern hemisphere.

Give it a shot yourself if you don't believe me. A guy with *two* PhDs tried and even he couldn't do it. He posted online—for the world to see if the world didn't have better things to do with its time—the following: "Suppose you buy a stock at $10. It goes up to $50 and then down to $5. You've lost 450 percent." Nope. Your stock has gone from $10 to $5, a fifth-grade textbook case of a 50 percent decline.

The *100 percent* rule is a rule of math, and as mentioned earlier, rules of math are strictly enforced. That means the web page in Figure 3.1 is wrong.

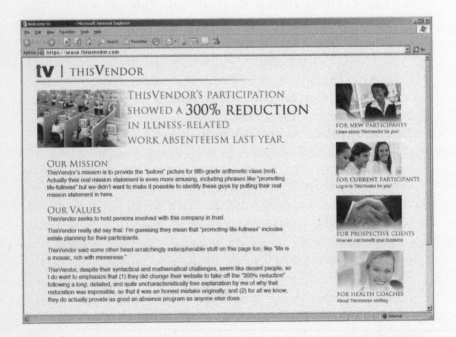

Figure 3.1 Example of (since-removed) Vendor Website Not Constrained by Conventional Rules of Math*

---

*After a conversation lasting much longer than it should have, I was able to convince these guys of the 100 percent rule, and now their website is accurate, with "accurate" being defined as "not outside the theoretical realm of possibility for a change."

It's lucky math isn't a popularity contest because these guys aren't the only ones who think you can reduce a number by more than 100 percent, as the conclusion of this case study from Vendor D suggests: "Wellness program participants are **225% less likely** [boldface is actually theirs, believe it or not] to utilize Extended Illness Benefit than non-participants." Note that for copyright reasons (even though this brochure wasn't copyrighted) both the hospital's name and the percentage reduction were changed. We did them a favor not just on the former but also on the latter, because the actual number they claimed was even higher.

It's Lucky Arithmetic Is Not a Popularity Contest Because Here Is Another Vendor Whose Outcomes Break the Mathematical Impossibility Barrier

Wellness Program Case Study: St. Mary's Hospital

St. Mary's Hospital started their [sic] first comprehensive wellness program in 2006, implementing a personalized approach focused around a high trust, high engagement strategy with [Vendor D]. The following provides data directly from that program.

Sick Time

> *Like most organizations, hours tied to sick time are categorized as Extended Illness Benefit (EIB). Anomalies such as maternal leave were pulled out, leaving 96 percent of the population for the analysis. The result was that **wellness program participants are 225 percent less likely to utilize EIB** than non-participants.*

Maybe "225 percent" wasn't enough to excite their customers because the Vendor D website now proclaims "390 percent" (See Figure 3.2.).

Figure 3.2   Besides Being Mathematically Impossible, What Does This Even Mean?

It's hard to tell which makes less sense: the numbers or the words. "390 percent" compared to what? There is also a misplaced modifier issue, as in "crossing the street, the bus hit me." Or, perhaps they intended it to read this way. Perhaps the "400 percent losses" apply only to "employers associated with chronic disease," such as Merck, Pfizer, and maybe Healthways or Alere. Presumably, being in the chronic disease business, they can make up their mathematically impossible losses in volume. The good news is that NASA employees don't need to worry about their job security, because these people are obviously not rocket scientists.

However, even highly respected organizations can trip over the 100 percent rule. Here is a press release citing the Institute for Healthcare Improvement (IHI). The consensus would be that IHI is one of the most capable and influential organizations in the field. And yet . . .

PCMH Effectiveness: The Proof Is In

HI-WIRE George Miller January 04, 2010

*A five-year prospective evaluation of the model yields a 129 percent increase in patients receiving optimal diabetes care and a 48 percent increase for heart-disease patients. The model also achieved a **350 percent reduction** in appointment waiting time, as reported by the Institute for Healthcare Improvement.*

More common violations of the *100 percent* rule are not as flagrant. As a reader of these reports you can't assume that your vendors will simply *announce* that they are violating basic rules of fifth-grade arithmetic. You will have to infer it. Here is an example, and there will be plenty more in the case studies.

The Center for Health Value Innovation The Center for Health Value Innovation (CHVI) has a vision statement that says, "[CHVI] will be the trusted resource to demonstrate how engagement in health can improve accountability and economic performance." In one of their presentations they showed a savings of $5,000 per person per year (net savings, meaning *after* fees are subtracted) generated by a care management program for commercially insured members, where this number was said to be for the "average" person. However, the average commercially insured person doesn't even *incur* $5,000/year in paid claims—and certainly not in claims that could be considered even theoretically avoidable—making it impossible to reduce claims by this amount, especially net of fees—a clear violation of the *100 percent* rule.

An example like this demonstrates the need for more instruction in the health outcomes numeracy field, both in general and also specifically because the CHVI, which itself provides instruction in outcomes-based contracting, was unable to recognize it is not possible to save $5,000/year/person in a commercial population.

The *Every Metric Can't Improve* Rule: Every Element of Resource Use or Group of People Cannot Decline in Cost through Programs Aimed Generally at Improving Prevention. In Particular, the Actual Costs Associated with Prevention, Such as Primary Care Visits, Drug Use, and Health Screening, Must Rise

The *Why Nobody Believes* mantra: If you insulate your house, you should save money overall, but you won't save money on insulation.

Likewise, in healthcare you need to spend more money in some areas to save money overall. So, for instance, unless you believe it's possible to talk people out of taking their drugs and have their inpatient utilization decline nonetheless, this Health Plan C slide has face impossibility (not to mention that the quantities in the first two columns don't sum to the quantity in the last column of Figure 3.3).

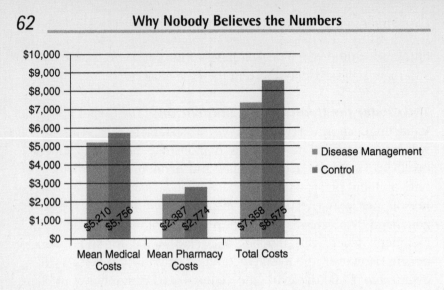

FIGURE **3.3** Cost/Year of Members in DM Program versus Control Group

One might hypothesize that the pre-post phenomenon described earlier in this book might be responsible for the outcomes, given that Health Plan C uses the pre-post methodology and doesn't do plausibility checks. The result could also have been caused by comparing people who volunteered to participate in the program to those who didn't participate—a classic fallacy. This fallacy has already been noted, and is specifically covered later under the *control group equivalency* rule. And we will bring it up a bunch more times before the book is done.

Once again, the in-depth case studies will show more examples in more detail.

THE *50 PERCENT SAVINGS* RULE: IN A VOLUNTARY HEALTH MANAGEMENT PROGRAM WITH NO INCENTIVES, DECLINES IN EXCESS OF 50 PERCENT IN ANY GIVEN RESOURCE CATEGORY ARE THE RESULT OF INVALIDITY, NOT EFFECTIVENESS

Years of doing valid outcomes measurement have confirmed the obvious: You can't "move the needle" a lot without strong financial incentives. Want people to stay out of the ER? Sure, you can entice doctors to keep longer hours by paying them more, and that should reduce ER usage a little bit. Double the ER co-pay, though, and watch ER visits decline.

You *especially* can't move the needle on chronic disease events, because most adverse events simply aren't preventable with a few outbound phone calls.

And in reality, the needle-moving impossibility threshold, using programs without strong economic incentives/disincentives, is more like 20 percent. I chose 50 percent because there are so many outcomes studies showing greater improvements than that.

Georgia Medicaid   State agencies routinely accept outcomes that violate one or more of the plausibility rules, as we will see in-depth in the next chapter, and again in Chapter 8. Here is an example from Georgia Medicaid, prepared by Benefits Consulting Firm A. A word-for-word reconstruction of the summary page of their report follows:

The results of the reconciliation process for the guaranteed net savings in PY1 are highlighted below:

- In Region 1, Vendor E generated net savings, after subtracting their contracted fees, of 19.0 percent. These savings exceeded the contractually guaranteed net savings of 4.55 percent. No penalty should therefore be assessed for financial results.
- In Region 2, Vendor F generated net savings, after subtracting their contracted fees of 15.8 percent. These savings exceeded the contractually guaranteed net savings of 4.22 percent. No penalty should therefore be assessed for financial results.

The *50 percent savings* rule would guide readers to look at Region 1's 19 percent overall decrease. True, the *50 percent savings* rule focuses on declines of 50 percent or more, but that's 50 percent *in any single category*. A 19 percent overall decrease can—and will—easily be shown to require a >50 percent decline in hospitalizations, since disease management generates savings almost exclusively in hospital costs and ER costs, the latter being quite trivial, though, as compared to the former. (See the Appendix for numerical resource use details.) Because the idea of disease management is to provide enough preventive services and self-care to avoid hospitalizations, typically the cost of non-hospital services *increases* in successful programs. (Insulation, remember?)

Let us, however, generously assume away any likely increase in non-hospital costs and say that the hospitalization reduction was achieved *without* increasing prevention-oriented costs. Next, let us add back in the actual fees, approximately $9 per member per month or roughly 2 percent, making the gross savings before fees 21 percent (19 percent + 2 percent).

Let us also make some assumptions for program outreach and intervention effectiveness that are generous to the program in that they exceed, in most cases by a lot, what most programs achieve:

- Hospital costs account for 50 percent of total costs in the Medicaid disabled population (see the Appendix for a comparison to commercial populations).
- 50 percent of hospitalizations are avoidable through phone calls.
- 50 percent of people are engaged by the program.
- 50 percent of those engaged are (without financial incentives, which were not provided) successful enough in losing weight, giving up cigarettes, and taking other steps so that they do indeed avoid hospitalizations.

We can build these assumptions into a table to determine how many hospitalizations would need to be avoided in the last bullet-pointed group—the sub-category in which the program was effective—in order to save 21 percent gross, meaning 19 percent net plus the 2 percent fees.

Category	% of Total	Reduction in Costs Needed to Get 21% Overall Gross Savings
Hospital Costs	50% of costs are hospital costs	42% of total hospital costs must be avoided
Avoidable Hospital Costs	50% of hospital costs are avoidable through telephone disease management	84% of avoidable costs must be avoided
Engagement Rate	50% of members are engaged	168% of total hospital costs must be avoided in the engaged population
Success Rate	50% of engaged members are successful in avoiding avoidable hospitalizations	336% of avoidable hospitalizations must be avoided in the engaged population

Obviously, despite generous assumptions for contact and success rates in disease management, the 19 percent net savings result that the state of Georgia accepted is so obviously a violation of the *50 percent savings* rule that some might question whether the state's administrators at the time accepted the findings not because they believed them but rather because the results justified further federally matched spending on the program.

Postscript: Vendor E, having grossly underbid the project, was later found to have made almost no outgoing phone calls to beneficiaries, and consequently agreed to return money to the state.[1] So, Benefits Consulting Firm A was able to find mathematically impossible savings for the state despite the fact that the vendor allegedly generating those savings acknowledged not doing anything. (Benefits Consulting Firm A is not alone in believing that savings can be found without improving the population. As we will see in Chapter 4, Vendor D says that with their program you can save $340/person/year on people whose risk factors simply stay the same.)

Illinois Medicaid   What list of states lying about finances would be complete without Illinois? Here is their press release, which claims more savings through disease management than the state actually spent on chronic disease events, a *100 percent* rule and a poster child for face impossibility. (Oh, yes, and in actuality their chronic disease events did not even decline enough to pay for the program, a minor detail.) But some other bigger news at the time about that state's governor relegated this news to the inside pages, sort of like Michael Jackson's death did to Farrah Fawcett's.

Illinois' Care Management Programs Save $320 Million in Successful Third Year

Programs result in effective coordination of services, better health outcomes and cost savings

SPRINGFIELD—Today the Illinois Department of Healthcare and Family Services (HFS) announced $320 million in savings in fiscal year 2009, the third year of operations for two popular care management programs, *Illinois Health Connect* and *Your Healthcare Plus.*

"When we are able to effectively teach individuals how to manage their illnesses and coordinate with a medical home, it leads to fewer emergency room and hospital visits, which in turn reduces costs and most importantly improves the quality of life for each individual," said HFS Director Julie Hamos. "As Illinois and the nation move toward implementing national Healthcare reform, we intend to build on the success of *Illinois Health Connect* and *Your Healthcare Plus* and to strengthen our health information technology infrastructure, which provides the foundation for successful care management."

THE *NEXUS* RULE: THERE MUST BE A LOGICAL LINK BETWEEN THE GOAL OF THE PROGRAM AND THE SOURCE OF SAVINGS

Listen carefully once again: You can only achieve savings in the categories in which you are trying to achieve savings. If costs decline in any other category, it had nothing to do with you. We will see two examples in our detailed case studies of this, but for now, consider this slide. We can't say the name of—or even assign a code name to and then charge you for revealing the name of—the vendor shown in Figure 3.4 because this slide wasn't published, but that doesn't make it any less amusing.

It's not just that everything declines. It's that the biggest declines are in the two largely preventive categories (*MD visits* and *drugs*) where one would expect an increase—exactly contradicting the tenets of care management. Yes, once again that goes back to the observation that even if insulating your house saves money, the cost of the insulation itself doesn't decline.

Perhaps Ned Flanders would be okay with this type of internal inconsistency because he believes everything in the Bible, including the "stuff that contradicts the other stuff" but obviously no one else would, right? Wrong. For three years these guys presented this material without anyone other than me noticing. To their credit, they

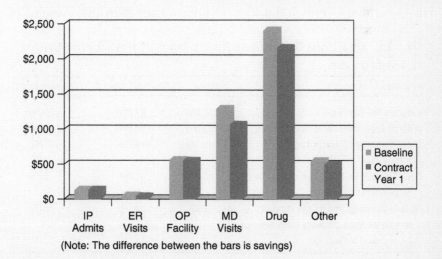

(Note: The difference between the bars is savings)

FIGURE 3.4 Savings by Category of Utilization per 1,000 Members per Month

did change their methodologies after I suggested doing so for the third time.*

THE *QUALITY DOSE–COST RESPONSE* RULE: JUST AS IN PHARMACOLOGY, WHERE THERE IS AN OBSERVABLE TIME-DEPENDENT RELATIONSHIP BETWEEN DOSE AND RESPONSE, COST CANNOT DECLINE SIGNIFICANTLY FASTER OR MORE THAN THE RELATED QUALITY VARIABLES IMPROVE

There is no way that events can decline if you don't improve quality. If they do, that's face impossibility. Usually the changes in quality variables are a smoking gun that invalidates the entire cost savings claim, as in Table 3.1.

Along with a lack of understanding of significant digits, percentages versus decimals, and changes in percentage versus changes in percentage points, this example clearly shows what is sometimes informally referred to in population health improvement as the "wishful thinking multiplier":

% Event or Cost Reduction/% Improvement in Quality Indicators

Or, in wellness:

% Cost Reduction /% Risk Factor Reduction

In this example, the wishful thinking multiplier is about 40, meaning that events fell about 40 times faster than the average of

TABLE **3.1** How Trivial Quality Improvements Generate Massive Reductions in Hospitalizations

% Cardiac Members	Base	Contract Year 1	*Improvement*
With an LDL screen	75.0%	77.0%	*2.0%*
With at least one claim for a statin	69.0%	70.5%	*1.5%*
Receiving an ACE inhibitor or alternative	43.5%	44.7%	*1.2%*
Post-MI with at least one claim for a beta-blocker	0.89	0.89	*0.0%*
Hospitalizations per 1,000 cardiac members for a primary diagnosis of myocardial infarction	47.60	24.38	*−48.8%*

---

*They say the third time's a charm.

those four quality variables improved. The *real* wishful thinking multiplier, as we will see when we review the valid literature and review "mediation analysis" that connects the two, is only slightly greater than 0 for the first two to three years of a program.

Even the denominator itself can be gamed, whether quality indicators or risk factors. Let's start with quality indicators. Several vendors are partial to bragging that "10 of the 15 quality indicators either improved or stayed the same." That means five deteriorated. If, of the 10 that improved or stayed the same, half stayed the same, as is often the case, no quality improvement took place. Five indicators got better and five got worse.

One of the vendor community's favorite tools involving quality indicators is a "gaps in care" report, like this one in Figure 3.5.

The vendor reports that 43 percent of open care gaps were closed, while only 19 percent of closed care gaps opened up. Big success, right? Look again. This time, focus on the absolute number of gaps that changed over the course of the year. Turns out, there was virtually no change in open care gaps.

The wellness equivalent of quality indicator improvement, risk factor reduction, is equally if not more suspect and will be addressed in the wellness vignettes in the next chapter. It turns out that alleged risk factor reduction is often the result of fallacious measurement

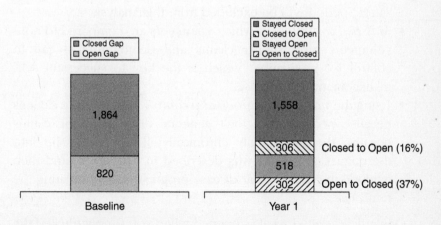

FIGURE 3.5 Changes in Care Gaps for Engaged Members with the Condition in the Baseline

rather than actual impact. For instance, many wellness vendors measure only the engaged (participating) members, meaning the ones most likely to comply. We see this particular fallacy about once every 10 pages. And often vendors measure only the people who showed up in the baseline, against themselves a year later. That "historic control" fallacy is described in the next section.

THE *CONTROL GROUP EQUIVALENCY* RULE: CONTROL GROUPS, IF NOT PROSPECTIVELY SORTED INTO TWO SIMILAR OR EQUIVALENT GROUPS, BASED ON OBJECTIVE DATA, BEFORE MEMBERS ARE EVEN CONTACTED TO DETERMINE WILLINGNESS TO ENROLL, ARE LIKELY TO MISLEAD. THIS IS ESPECIALLY TRUE OF *HISTORIC CONTROLS* (MEANING PRE–POST), *MATCHED CONTROLS*, AND *USING THE NON–DISEASE GROUP AS A CONTROL FOR THE DISEASE GROUP*

One reason that there is a rule covering multiple violations is that you tend not to get impossible results without making myriad mistakes along the way. So many of the control group equivalency fallacies were covered earlier, or will be part of the in-depth Case Studies in Cluelessness Gone Wild. Some footage from the highlights reel:

◆ *Historic controls*—meaning the same population before and after—creates a fallacy where people who were high-cost enough to make it into your "before" population will as a group regress to the mean, but formerly low-cost people not in the "before" population who regress upwards during the "after" period will be excluded from this analysis.

◆ *Matched controls*—in which volunteers are compared to non-volunteers with similar claims and demographics—fail to control for motivation, which is the key to successful self-management of a disease.

◆ Using the *non-disease group as a control* will overstate savings because people who don't generate disease-specific claims because they are mildly chronically ill will often slip into the control group, as was described in Chapter 1, and then explode in costs as their disease progresses, thus inflating the trend line.

One article[2] traced what happened when you simply tracked the costs of people who were identified in the baseline year absent a

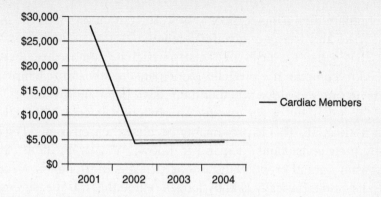

FIGURE 3.6   Cost by Change in Cardiac Members by Year

program—a historic control. (Note that the study used a very tight algorithm to identify cardiac patients—a cardiac event in the baseline year. See Figure 3.6. The broader the algorithm, the more muted the heads-to-tails effect.)

Consider perhaps the best pure example of failure to control for motivation by using matched controls, taken verbatim from the white paper downloadable from the website of Vendor G:

♦ "We utilize an opt-in enrollment model to target those individuals who have high health confidence and the highest motivation to change their health situation," and so as not to leave anything to chance, Vendor G then . . .

♦ ". . . provides incentives to participants in our Condition Management Programs."

Farther down on their website, they note that they produce "valuable disease management reports" that "provide you with ROI."

How do these "valuable disease management reports" determine an ROI? To what control group do they compare motivated, incentivized volunteers? They "match members in the measurement year with non-participating members with similar clinical, utilization, and cost characteristics." In other words, they do precisely what a biostatistician or health services researcher would never do: They find (1) motivated volunteers, (2) bribe them to participate, and then

(3) compare the results to people who lacked enough motivation to participate and were not given incentives.

What is their justification? "This approach is used because there is a need to compare the program participants to *something* [emphasis theirs] in order to judge whether there have been improvements." In other words, they prefer to offer an obviously invalid ROI analysis than none at all. This is presumably because their customers, egged on by their consultants, demand to know: "What's my ROI?" Yep, they want a number, notwithstanding that it is meaningless. Vendor G, to its credit, basically acknowledges online that this measurement is meaningless, and provides it only because their customers are insisting on it.

THE *MULTIPLE VIOLATIONS* RULE: WHEN ONE OF THESE RULES IS VIOLATED, OTHERS ARE LIKELY TO BE VIOLATED, AS WELL

This is an excellent segue into Chapter 4, both because we will highlight multiple violations of the *multiple violations* rule, and also because we are now done with Chapter 3.

Chapter 4

Case Studies That Flunk Every Plausibility Test Known to Mankind and Then Some

Health Plan H, Benefits Consulting Firm A, a Red State spending taxpayer money like a Blue State, and a pretty big chunk of the wellness industry. In each case, we will dissect purported outcomes or promises they themselves have published. In each case, we will highlight those alleged outcomes/promises against a background of fifth-grade math to allow you, the reader, now educated in plausibility, to judge their veracity.

While many of us would acknowledge some prurient interest in watching self-anointed experts stumble over basic arithmetic, epidemiology, and integrity, the point of all these examples is actually to learn how to measure outcomes correctly. And the chapters following this one will highlight examples of outcomes reports measured correctly. Perhaps surprising readers who will have been just weaned on these Case Studies in Cluelessness Gone Wild, those subsequent chapters will show *actual savings,* bringing to mind the immortal words of the great philosopher Basil Fawlty: "A satisfied customer. Let us have him stuffed and mounted."

Case Study #1: Achieving Dramatic Reductions in Risk Factors and Medical Spending by Implementing Off-the-Shelf Wellness Programs (*Not*)

So little has been documented about wellness that even the size of the industry is a mystery.[1] Nonetheless, its apparent popularity suggests that it is the largest, fastest-growing, unstudied segment of healthcare services. Throw in a pending government subsidy for small employers to undertake wellness programs, and it seems like now would be a good time to figure out whether wellness actually works.

The hypothesis behind wellness programs is that helping employees to improve their health habits will reduce rates of smoking and obesity (and other risk factors), thereby reducing healthcare utilization and improving productivity. Studies, albeit incorporating many design shortcomings acknowledged by the authors of the meta-analysis, have supported this hypothesis,[2] and some companies, like Health Plan B, guarantee a reduction in these rates.

Maybe companies can generate savings over a longer time frame by reducing risk and maybe they can't. Unfortunately, with the exception of one well-designed trial described below, we'll never know: In wellness, the basis of competition seems to be to claim (or, in Health Plan B's case, guarantee) the best results the fastest, rather than to counsel employers to be patient and diligent to possibly achieve valid albeit modest results through hard work over a longer time frame, consistent with that trial.

And why describe valid albeit unexciting outcomes when the marketplace lacks the sophistication to distinguish valid from invalid claims, allowing the latter to proliferate? There is a law in economics: *Bad money drives out good*. Its corollary in wellness: *Bad outcomes methodologies drive out good ones*. It's tough to compete on the basis of valid outcomes when one's competitors are touting impossibly good ones, and benefits consultants can't distinguish between the two.

To analyze risk outcomes and their effect on healthcare costs, one must—at a bare minimum—understand grade-school arithmetic,* risk factors, the relationship between risk factors and cost reduction, and the necessity of conclusions being at least slightly plausible. Many vendors, despite flunking one or more of those entry-level requirements, thrive because many customers are oblivious to this failure.

HEALTH PLAN B'S LAKE WOBEGON WELLNESS GUARANTEE: MISUNDERSTANDING OR MISCOMMUNICATING THE WAY RISK FACTORS WORK

An individual's risk factors do not stand still. We are not born as obese smokers. At some point in our lives, some of us gain weight, while others take up smoking. Likewise, we often take successful steps on our own to reduce or eliminate these and other risk factors. The improvement in risk factors may be temporary or permanent. The University of Michigan's Dee Edington quantified these changes in risk factors into what he termed *the natural flow of risk*,[3] in which, among other movements over a three-year period:

- 35 percent of high-risk people become medium-risk.
- 40 percent of medium-risk people become low-risk.
- 33 percent of low-risk people become high- or medium-risk.

Yet, Health Plan B, which boasts that it has based its wellness program on "30 years of research by Dee Edington," markets its product as though Dr. Edington's research didn't exist. Health Plan B's "Better Health Guarantee" promises employers a "30 percent reduction in risk among high- and medium-risk employees" if

---

*The most frequent basic arithmetic error is failure to understand that a number may not be reduced by more than 100 percent, as noted earlier in this book. The fact that this happens at all—and no one notices, and these companies are successful—means readers and their consultants have to be much more vigilant in reviewing all vendor claims.

75 percent complete a health risk assessment (HRA), displayed in their brochure, as follows, as seen in Figure 4.1.

Note that the "guaranteed" 30 percent risk reduction is gross, not net—the down-arrows only, a clear violation of the *control group equivalency* rule because people are their own historic controls. The display shows no up-arrows for the low-risk people migrating to higher risk categories, even though Dee Edington's 30 years of research clearly demonstrates that risk flows in both directions. A look at the Edington numbers above shows that Health Plan B's guarantee is a safe bet (for Health Plan B, not their customers) if only the gross reduction in risk for the high- and medium-risk employees is counted.*

Suppose high and medium-risk members are "heads" and low-risk members are *tails*. This is what Health Plan B is promising in Figure 4.2.

Health Plan B is guaranteeing that a certain percentage of heads will flip to tails, an outcome that the Edington research concludes would eventually happen anyway. Wouldn't the valid promise include tails-to-heads migration to offset heads-to-tails, which, according to Edington and common sense, also happens? The brochure—despite Edington's research to the contrary–seems to be ignoring the possibility of the following migration seen in Figure 4.3.

So, Health Plan B is quick to take credit for the random heads flipping over to tails, but does not mention the random tails flipping over to heads. How does this omission of tails-to-heads affect the validity of the metrics? An easy test of the validity of the Health Plan B guarantee would be to assume (1) only one risk factor,

---

*A book about inaccuracy needs to be accurate. Therefore, it is important to note that the Dee Edington risk migration from high-risk to medium- and low-risk, and is calculated over a longer time frame than the Health Plan B guarantee. Consequently, the high-risk population would need to improve at a rate faster than Dee Edington's three-year rate in order for Health Plan B to achieve its guaranteed reduction. For instance, suppose over the 14 months listed in Health Plan B's brochure as the guarantee period, only 25 percent of people would enjoy declining risk factors on their own. Health Plan B would then have to improve another 5 percent for real, in order to hit a 30 percent target.

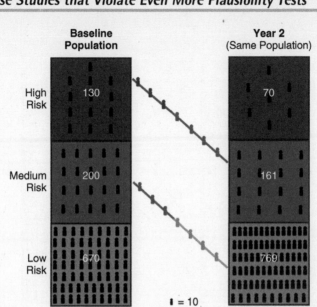

FIGURE 4.1 The Lake Wobegon Risk Reduction Guarantee

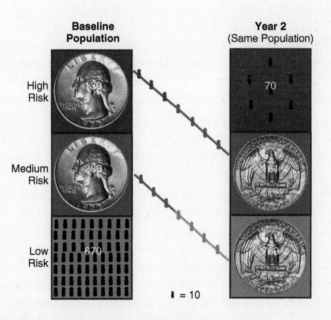

FIGURE 4.2 Heads-and-Tails Meets Lake Wobegon

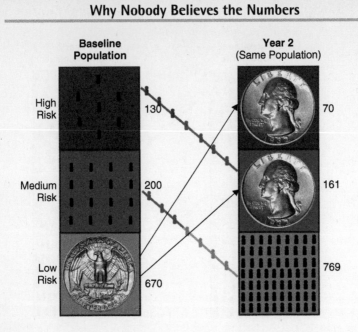

FIGURE 4.3   Tails Migrating to Heads

current smoking; and (2) that everyone in an organization smokes and quits for a year at a time. Therefore, at the beginning of the Health Plan B program an HRA would reveal a 50 percent current smoking rate, and only those 50 percent would be counted for the pre-post result. In this hypothetical in which people stop smoking annually on their own anyway, Health Plan B achieves a 100 percent risk reduction even without doing anything, because at the time of the next HRA, everyone who was previously smoking and hence high-risk is no longer smoking and hence no longer high-risk.

That next HRA will show a 50 percent smoking rate, too: The *other* 50 percent of the population—who had not been smoking and hence were low-risk ("tails"), and therefore not counted, at the time of the previous HRA—are now smoking. Health Plan B will now count them as high-risk, now that they have already flipped on their own to "heads". A year later they will have quit, creating another banner year for the Health Plan B program, which will report a 100 percent risk reduction, using its guarantee methodology.

This process could continue *ad infinitum*, with Health Plan B reporting 100 percent quit rates in each cycle while the rate of smoking remains at 50 percent.

One might ask, how could Health Plan B, having studied Dee Edington's 30 years of research, and presumably having actuaries capable of doing the simple proof above nonetheless fail to understand the way risk factors work, in such a manner as to inadvertently grossly overstate its performance in order to achieve its guarantees?

Is it possible that they know how risk factors work, and that they instead decided that their brochure would feature the three risk segments not drawn to scale in their bar chart, in order to divert attention from the low-risk segment on the bottom, the one-third of the chart in which two-thirds of the population resides?

Only people within Health Plan B know the answer to that question. There can only be two explanations. Health Plan B wants to do one of two things:

1. Offer a fair guarantee but does not understand the flow of risk or how to draw a bar chart
2. Focus its customers and their consultants on gross risk reduction and hope that they don't notice or understand the omission of the risk-increase offsets from the low-risk population

Despite the other questions being raised, one line on the cover of the brochure would be very hard to challenge. This is indeed "A Promise Only [Health Plan B] Can Make."

So Health Plan B Lies About Its Outcomes to Its Customers, Right?

It would be so much more fun to say "yes" and fume with righteous indignation, but quite the contrary: They are about the only ones who tell the truth. Really. When Health Plan B reports its wellness outcomes, it conscientiously tracks exactly

(continued)

(*continued*)

what Dee Edington says should be tracked—the flow of risk in all directions, not just the number of people whose risk factors declined. It's a delicate balancing act for Health Plan B, to gently re-educate customers on valid measurement in order to reset expectations without blowing up the whole relationship. Imagine the Outcomes Fairy-meets-*The Hurt Locker*.

This methodology, paradoxically, puts Health Plan B in the very top echelon of integrity and validity in wellness reporting. Not that there is much competition for that distinction among health plans, as the examples from Health Plan H and Health Plan I show.

Come to think of it, there isn't much competition for integrity and validity *anywhere* in this field, as the next ten vignettes will show . . . and that's exactly why there is a discrepancy between Health Plan B's guarantees and their outcomes. As one Health Plan B executive put it: "In order to compete, industry standard metrics and guarantees must be utilized to get in the door. Once we're inside and the customer trusts us, we educate people on validity, and note that all ROI claims are not created equal. But if we didn't play the guaranteed outcomes game to begin with, we wouldn't have the opportunity to set people straight."

THE WISHFUL THINKING MULTIPLIER: THE SIZE AND TIMING OF THE WELLNESS PROGRAM PAYBACK

Arguably the most carefully designed study to determine the effect of wellness programs on cost was done on the employees of Highmark Blue Cross over a multi-year period.[4] One of the leading academic wellness researchers, Ron Goetzel, was involved in this study, so you know it's good. Truth be told, Ron's analysis is much better

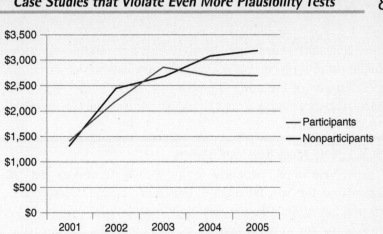

FIGURE 4.4 Highmark Wellness Program Annual Claims Cost per Employee (versus Program Participation)

than mine.* This study found that cost improvement lagged wellness program implementation by several years, as noted in Figure 4.4. The study did (by necessity) compare participants to non-participants, but the fact that the two groups trended together for three years means they probably were comparable.

VENDOR K: IMMEDIATE SAVINGS

In sharp and no doubt coincidentally self-serving contrast, programs proposed by vendors almost invariably show results over a much shorter time frame. For instance, Vendor K's website features a case study in which participants' health expenses increased 17.3 percentage points more slowly than non-participants *in the first year*, even though risk factors for high- and medium-risk participants declined only 3 percent and 5.5 percent respectively during that year. Comparing the 17.3 percent savings to the average risk factor decline of 4.25 percent gives Vendor K a wishful thinking multiplier of

---

*You weren't expecting that, were you? In my defense I would say his analyses cost ten times what mine cost, but they're not ten times better. Also, my analyses use shorter words, so they emit less CO_2.

about 4:1. Note also that, as usual, participants are compared to non-participants and—recall the Health Plan B discussion—no allowance is made for low-risk employees whose risk factors deteriorate. That's two violations of the *control group equivalency* rule—(1) failing to control for motivation and (2) using high/medium-risk people as their own control.

VENDOR L: EVEN MORE IMMEDIATE SAVINGS

At least Vendor K patiently waits for the earth to get all the way around the sun before touting their savings. Vendor L boasts 22.5 percent savings *in the first eight month*s of a program. Vendor L reports on its website savings of 15 percent in the first year in a client's program even though the program wasn't implemented until May of that year. This means that the May to December savings for the first year would have needed to reach 22.5 percent, to achieve 15 percent for the year as a whole. To put this in perspective, consider a typical corporate medical spending scenario, in which about a quarter of all costs are non-surgical, non-birth event inpatient expenses. In that case, remaining hospital utilization—including hospitalizations for non-participants—would have to fall almost to zero starting the day of program implementation. (See Appendix for a typical breakout of inpatient expenses.) Here's a surprise: Vendor L's website did not provide inpatient utilization statistics to back up its savings claims.

Vendor L No Stranger to Difficult Undertakings

In addition to this performance, Vendor L's website says that "in an actual client case study" Vendor L was able to "demonstrate the potential savings for the client if each of their members was [sic] to eliminate one risk factor." Remarkable! An *actual* case study showing *potential* savings! Where do I sign?

IT'S A BIRD. IT'S A PLANE. IT'S VENDOR M

Just like Superman saved Lois Lane by making the earth spin backwards, Vendor M shows savings *even before the program starts*.

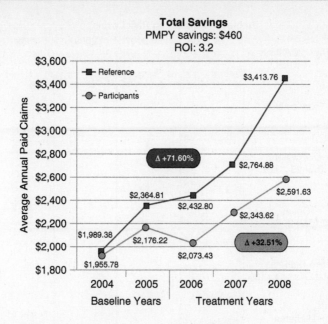

FIGURE 4.5 Achieving Savings Before the Program Starts

Figure 4.5 of Vendor M's performance at Eastman Chemical shows an 8 percent relative improvement for participants in Year 2 of the baseline, before the participants even had the opportunity to participate.

Vendor M also throws in a violation of the *quality dose–cost response* rule, as their financial savings far exceed the percentage improvements in the risk levels. When one averages the six risk score improvements they highlighted (Figure 4.6), and adds in the two risk factors they didn't mention because they didn't improve, one gets an average risk factor improvement of about 15 percent.

The savings was about 24 percent, so the wishful thinking multiplier was "only" about 1.6x. What makes this result implausible isn't so much the wishful thinking multiplier itself (though that, too) but rather the sheer magnitude of the savings. The Appendix lists components of spending and utilization in general. A quick glance at it shows that it simply isn't possible to save 24 percent in claims cost, through wellness or anything else.

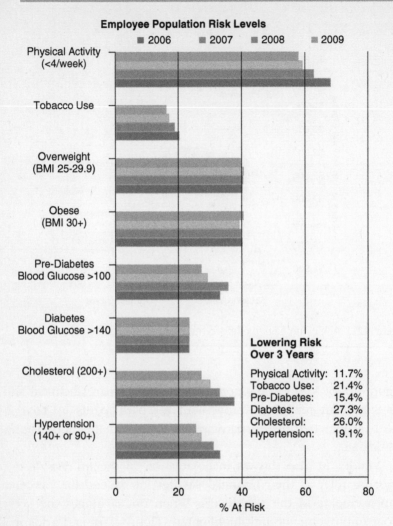

Employee Population Risk Levels
■ 2006   ■ 2007   ■ 2008   ■ 2009

Physical Activity (<4/week)

Tobacco Use

Overweight (BMI 25-29.9)

Obese (BMI 30+)

Pre-Diabetes Blood Glucose >100

Diabetes Blood Glucose >140

Cholesterol (200+)

Hypertension (140+ or 90+)

Lowering Risk Over 3 Years

Physical Activity:	11.7%
Tobacco Use:	21.4%
Pre-Diabetes:	15.4%
Diabetes:	27.3%
Cholesterol:	26.0%
Hypertension:	19.1%

0   20   40   60   80
% At Risk

FIGURE 4.6   Quality Improvements at Eastman Chemical

Why the Wishful Thinking Multiplier Is Called the Wishful Thinking Multiplier: Doing the Math

First, a big thank-you to Ariel Linden, PhD, cited previously in *Why Nobody Believes the Numbers*. He is one of the two evaluators in the wellness field (Ron Goetzel being the other) who not only do not require adult supervision, but could provide it, not just to others but probably to me as well in some of the nuances of the field. Ariel is introducing the PHI field to the concept—well known in *real* health services research—of mediation analysis, the mathematical/epidemiological link between behavior change and cost savings.

To simplify his insights greatly, suppose there is a risk factor—let's call it cholesterol—where the difference between good and bad is a 25 percent increase in heart attack risk. Suppose further that a program reduces the number of people with bad cholesterol levels by 20 percent, which would be huge. In real life the change in heart attack incidence from this reduction isn't purely linear or immediate, but directionally what I'm about to say is true: heart attacks in that population would decline 4 percent. 4 percent is 20 percent times 25 percent: a 20 percent reduction in the number of people with the risk factor times 25 percent—the impact of the risk factor on heart attack rates.

Thus, the wishful thinking multiplier in real life—even if this reduction happened in the first year—would be far below 1x: a 4 percent reduction in an event rate whose cost consumes at most 5 percent of healthcare spending. That's so far below 1x that I need to do the math: 4 percent of 5 percent is 0.2 percent.

That 0.2 percent is then divided by the risk factor reduction of 20 percent to yield a wishful thinking multiplier of 0.01x.

And that's for a *successful* program, assuming the cholesterol reduction takes place right away and impacts heart attacks right away.

In all fairness, it is possible that cholesterol reduction reduces some other event risk, and/or that the program improves some other variables not being measured that have an indirect effect

(continued)

(continued)

on heart attacks as well. Suppose that situation is the case, and that somehow we missed *90 percent* of the indirect effect of the wellness program on cost. That would bring the wishful thinking multiplier all the way up to . . . 0.1x.

Now you see why all these massive first-year cost reductions and wishful thinking multipliers are, to put it politely, controversial.

Think about your own medical spending: How much of it do you attribute to your own bad health habits that you think you might be motivated to change? In my case, being well *costs* my insurer money, as I end up with myriad injuries caused by some young whippersnapper crashing into me on the Ultimate Frisbee field, injuries that I would have avoided by sitting in front of a television and waiting for Medicare to pick up my tab starting in 2021.*

VENDOR D ENCORE: THE SEINFELD APPROACH TO WELLNESS SAVINGS

Vendor D's savings are about: *nothing*. Yes, your employees can save you money in the first year simply by doing nothing.

For those of you keeping score at home, that would be an *infinite* wishful thinking multiplier, as the $340 savings is divided by a risk factor reduction of 0 percent. To put this in perspective, my health plan premium was $3,400/year 10 years ago. Since my risk factors have stayed the same since then, my healthcare should now be free, right?

The bottom line is, while there are obvious marketing benefits to claiming immediate or (in the case of Vendor D) automatic savings to impress prospective customers who aren't reading this book, if the Highmark study teaches anything, it's patience: Wellness programs

---

*Even with those injuries, my healthcare costs are still much lower than the average for the demographic cohort that routinely uses the word "whippersnapper."

FIGURE 4.7 Vendor D Announcing Savings of $340/Year on Each Employee "Who Does Not Increase Their [sic] Risk Factors"

need time to work, and even then the savings against all spending will be in the single digits net of program expense. Consider all the intermediate steps between implementation and savings:

1. People must be apprised of the program's existence.
2. They need to be "sold" on it and convinced to take an HRA.
3. And/or maybe a health fair is scheduled for sometime thereafter.
4. Once people take the HRA and see their risk factors, they need to be convinced to undertake coaching.
5. A course of coaching or other behavior change is implemented.
6. Risk factors begin to improve.
7. Fewer events and other consequences happen, due to the improved risk profile, thus saving money.

This all assumes no backsliding in health habits, employee turnover is limited, and that changes to the high-risk population's risk profile are above and beyond the aforementioned "natural flow."

VENDOR N: THE CLAIMS THAT DIDN'T GET DETECTED IN THE NIGHTTIME (OR DAYTIME)

"Holmes, Vendor N says they saved $4 million in 'undetected claims cost' just on the highest-cost members. That is very impressive."

"Watson, you see but you do not observe. The most common mistake in wellness is to present conclusions that are mathematically or epidemiologically impossible. The distinction is clear. Vendor N's website says that the most expensive 2 percent of the employees of

Cumulus Media avoided about $72,000 apiece—in so-called 'undetected claims cost.' This has Moriarty's fingerprints all over it. Claims costs that don't get incurred because they aren't detected. No doubt those claims are making their way into Moriarty's pocket."

"You cannot detect them, Holmes? But you are the world's greatest detective."

"Indeed perhaps I am not, if I cannot detect undetected claims cost and Vendor N can. Or at least Vendor N has benefits consultants believing that impossible arithmetic is possible. If Moriarty has invented a way to control our wellness industry through Vendor N so that benefits managers believe impossible results, he is making new rules of math. He could rewrite all the textbooks used in Grade 1 to Grade 6, in whatever those schools are called."

"Elementary, my dear Holmes."

"Watson, now what do you have for me?"

"Holmes, I have a lot of questions about how Vendor N detects undetected claims cost. Could they maybe be using those gadgets for finding coins on the beach? Or do the employees have to pass through a scanner every day, like Karen Silkwood and Meryl Streep? And if Vendor N did not avoid all those undetected claims, how would employees get reimbursed for them? Would they fill out claims forms using invisible ink?"

"I'll ask the questions, Watson. You get me the data. I can't make my bricks without clay. Tell me, Watson, what is the data?"

"The data, Holmes, is that they also avoid $37,000 apiece in 'undetected claims cost' for the medium-risk members. Quite an impressive wellness company."

"Watson, you ignorant slut. You see everything, but you fail to reason from what you see. $72,000 is much more than the top 2 percent of a company's employees would be predicted to *spend* in avoidable expenses in the year following their inclusion in the top 2 percent, and equates to about four avoided hospitalizations apiece. Add to that about $37,000 in 'undetected claims cost' avoided for the medium-risk members, and Vendor N is avoiding $21 million of 'undetected claims cost' for Cumulus Media.

"Here's the rub, Watson: Cumulus Media's total healthcare spending is only about $6 million/year. Therefore they can't have saved $21 million. When you have eliminated the impossible, whatever remains, however improbable, must be the truth. Another case solved. Another Moriarty plot foiled. Math is saved for future generations to enjoy."

"Brilliant, Holmes. How do you do it?"

"You know my method, Watson. It is founded upon the observation of trifles, a little cocaine, and an occasional allusion to *Saturday Night Live*."

Cocaine may have been habit-forming for Mr. Holmes, but in Vendor N's case, impossibility seems to be habit-forming. The Scooter Score, another Vendor N customer, believes that their medical and drug claims declined 22 percent from 2009 to 2010 due to Vendor N's wellness program. Since only half the employees participated in the program, the 22 percent overall decline works out to a 44 percent reduction in costs for the 50 percent who did participate.

A 44 percent reduction in total costs for participants would wipe out all hospital and ER expense, including birth events for all participants, with no increase in drugs or preventive physician care to offset the reduction.

Viewed in a different way, the 22 percent overall reduction attributed to the wellness program exceeds the theoretical maximum avoidable by eliminating all admissions due to the AHRQ's list of ambulatory care-sensitive conditions (ACSC) for the 50 percent of employees who participated in the program ... while also eliminating all admissions for ACSC for the 50 percent who did not participate, along with roughly 1,000 of their closest friends.

And it was all achieved in the first year of the program. One wonders what they will do for an encore.

Aren't the employers' consultants supposed to be keeping this stuff from happening? Clearly the benefits consulting industry is not providing an effective check-and-balance. If the employers' benefits consultants could be trusted to distinguish real from invalid claims, then none of the statements above would still exist—the vendors would either need to correct them or go bankrupt. So what is the solution?

Well, at the risk of sounding like a broken record, you need to plausibility-test alleged outcomes that you are shown yourselves, using ingredients you already have in your kitchen.

These examples teach how to identify likely mistakes in vendor representations and guarantees. But it is more important to be able to plausibility-test all such claims, including the many that may be incorrect though not obviously so at first glance. Plausibility testing starts with the observation that it's not enough for costs or risk factors to appear to decline for participants. That decline could be due to the ubiquitous, albeit biostatistically discredited,[5] practice of comparing willing participants to non-participants—a violation of the *control group equivalency* rule. One cannot be sure whether self-selection rather than program impact caused the lower trend for willing participants.

Participant versus Nonparticipant Study Design: Beating This Horse Until Rigor Mortis Sets In

At the cost of killing a few more trees or (if you bought the e-copy) a few more electrons*, let us repeat yet again why you can't compare participants to nonparticipants.

Willingness to participate in anything is largely driven by motivation, and motivation is the #1 determinant of success in any voluntary self-help program. Therefore, you'd want to *control* for motivation in a study design, assigning similar proportions of motivated people to the study group as the control group.

Instead, having the study group be comprised solely of participants does exactly the opposite, thus predisposing a seemingly successful, but invalid result.

An extreme example would help. Suppose you wanted to show that getting people to run in triathlons would reduce heart disease. So you paid $100 to anyone who could complete a triathlon. Naturally, all of your employed triathletes would sign up for this program.

*Just for the record, I do actually know that reading e-books does not kill electrons, injure them, or for that matter even stress them out much. Indeed, with proper nutrition and exercise, they can live to be 100.

And guess what? Triathletes have much less heart disease than non-triathletes to begin with. So, just looking at the data, your conclusion would be that the incentive was successful in reducing heart disease by getting people to run in triathlons, since that group had less heart disease, when in reality all you did was pay the fittest people to do what they would have done anyway.

"Matching" the triathletes to a control group whose medical claims had also shown no evidence of heart disease prior to the race, but who declined to participate, would help just a little because your comparison group would exclude people with claims for pre-existing heart disease. However, unlike in the race group, at least some people in the matched-control group had just been lucky in avoiding heart disease (or maybe just hadn't been diagnosed with it yet), were not patrolling their health, and were not motivated enough to race for three hours for $100. Which group would you bet would be healthier going forward?

Obviously, no one would ever do this. And yet much more subtle examples of this get done all the time, like paying people to lose weight, stop smoking, etc. News flash: People who were *already considering* these interventions—or already doing them on their own—will sign up much faster than people who aren't, meaning the successes of participants may not be due to the program but rather to self-selection into the program.

There is a *right* way to match, but—yes, you're a step ahead—no one ever does it. You would offer the $100, get 100 people to sign up to race, and then tell 50 of them, otherwise equivalent to the other 50: "Here's your $100, but, sorry, you can't race." Train the others to race, presumably over multiple years, and compare the cardiac claims cost over time.

See how this example controls for motivation? Of course, it's very unlikely as a practical matter that any company would ever do this, but the mantra of this industry—see the Vendor G White Paper excerpt—is that it is better to design a study wrong than not at all.

Plausibility testing for wellness is even simpler than for disease management—and yet almost nobody does it.

First, to determine if your risk factors decline, run biometric screens on most if not all of your population and see whether the total number of risk factors declines noticeably between years. Don't rely solely on HRAs—way too subjective. Also, you can't simply count the people whose risk factors decline without counting those whose risk factors increased. That would be like estimating this year's increase in your net worth by simply adding your income this year to your net worth last year, without also adding in your annual expenses. Obvious, perhaps, and yet Health Plan B and Vendor K didn't do it.

Hence, the physical plausibility test must be mandatory (with exceptions on religious grounds), a biometric screen capturing all the major risk factors for all employees. There should be a noticeable reduction in risk factors once a wellness program is well underway. Remarkably—possibly because few people have focused on true valid wellness program measurement—no benchmarks exist for how much risk factors should decline population-wide at various intervals following wellness program implementation, and how that decline should vary with program expense and employee incentives. One thing is clear to everyone except Vendor D: Absence of noticeable change in risk factors means the program cannot be reducing health costs. (The reverse is not true, as the Highmark lag time demonstrates.)

If total companywide risk does decline, that by itself is a good thing and means your program is successful in the broadest sense of the word, if not financially. As the Highmark case study noted, that's about as far as you can go in the conclusion department, at least in the early years of a wellness program. If, however, someone is insisting that you look for a ROI, then run the same type of plausibility checks discussed in Chapter 2, but run them on conditions and resource uses that should be ameliorated by wellness. Measure all five event rates, plus specialist visits, ER visits, bariatric surgeries, and anything else you can think of that should decline if a population gets healthier.

That will constitute the visible portion of your savings attributable to reduced medical spending. You may have savings elsewhere, but use of these resources should noticeably decline. Otherwise, where did the savings come from? There is also savings due to improved productivity, which will be addressed in Chapter 8.

Remember, though, just as with disease management, wellness has to be measured on the *total population*. Just measuring on participants doesn't prove anything other than that participants are motivated. Whoopee. So, in the Vendor M example above, where 80 to 90 percent participated, the decline in events for the total population will capture the decline in events in participants, since the vast majority of Vendor M's customer Eastman Chemical participated. Eastman Chemical should be enjoying a massive reduction in adverse medical events, and resources like the ones listed above. But we'll never know because—with all the money they spent measuring outcomes and producing beautiful slides—they never bothered to ask themselves the basic question of whether health-sensitive medical events declined across their population.

It's a real head-scratcher that consultants or benefits managers don't insist on this, even though the savings being shown in many of the examples above and elsewhere are so far in excess of what could reasonably be expected that it would be impossible to achieve them *without* large declines in the inpatient events specifically associated with poor cardiometabolic health and/or smoking.

FEDERAL GOVERNMENT: PLAUSIBILITY-TEST AT A *MACRO* LEVEL AND DO A PROSPECTIVELY CONTROLLED TRIAL

Because employers seem willing to accept these wellness vendor claims instead of plausibility-testing them, it may fall to the federal government to educate employers, as they have done in disease management, increasing the sophistication of that marketplace.

What can the federal government do to validate its own planned subsidy for wellness programs for small businesses, using the same plausibility-test concept? The federal government already tracks potentially avoidable inpatient events in the insured population by state,[6] and the CDC already tracks smoking rates[7] and obesity[8] by state. Simply tracking wellness program uptake by state against those indicators (and controlling for increased tobacco taxes and other confounding state-level initiatives) will provide fodder for researchers to correlate and possibly assign causality.

A more sophisticated approach would be to run a prospective controlled study on federal employees, much like the government has done to test disease management, accountable care organizations and other interventions using Medicare recipients. (By the way, the federal government hasn't shown much in the way of results in those programs, either.)

Instead of comparing participants to nonparticipants, the groups would be divided in advance based on demographics and claims history. One group would be offered the program, the other group wouldn't. (One could work incentives into this study design as well, offering incentives to both groups but then not following through with a program for the control group.) Then the risk factors— and ultimately the costs—of the groups would be compared. This approach would provide easily the most rigorous data on wellness programs ever collected. Its results would have clear policy implications, both for the federal government's own employees as well as for subsidies offered to employers.

You see the difference between this proposal and the typical study design? The population is split into groups *before* people are asked if they want to participate. The two groups would have roughly equal numbers of motivated members, so a comparison of the groups would be valid.

Case Study #2: Raleigh, We Have a Problem

I've seen people spend more money on validation, and I've seen people do a worse job in validation, but I've never seen anyone spend more money on validation do a worse job in validation than North Carolina Medicaid. The provably false and generally impossible savings claims that their consultants generate have led states to redirect billions of dollars towards models like theirs, by showing results disconnected enough from reality to make the Outcomes Fairy blush. North Carolina is truly the Typhoid Mary of wasted Medicaid spending.

Further, as a result of these reports, the federal government, as we will see, is subsidizing this model heavily enough that one might call North Carolina Medicaid health care's Solyndra. The difference is that Solyndra eventually had to go bankrupt while North Carolina can keep making up numbers, at least until their subsidizers read this book.

North Carolina Medicaid is the model for 37 state Medicaid plans and many private-sector patient-centered medical home initiatives, and has been called the "poster child" for medical homes. However, the state has misstated all its major savings numbers. If you are a federal taxpayer, this is especially unfortunate because—partly due to the stated successes of the North Carolina program—the federal government now gives $9 to states for every $1 they spend implementing medical homes.[9]

By way of background, "patient-centered medical home (PCMH)" is defined, both in the Glossary but also right here (so the good news is, you don't have to look in the Glossary) as: "an approach to providing comprehensive primary care ... that facilitates partnerships between individual patients and their personal providers and, when appropriate, the patient's family."[10] There is widespread consensus on their role in the future of health reform, as represented by the Patient-Centered Primary Care Collaborative, an organization that has incorporated many stakeholders and has recently published a comprehensive White Paper on the subject, focused on the private sector, listing many small, well-contained studies in the private sector.[11]

The good news is patient satisfaction is quite high. That much, I can personally vouch for. I'm in a medical home and I love it. They're open seven days, waits to schedule an appointment are short (except, ironically, for periodic preventive physicals), and they have this completely cool electronic health record where, if I am so inclined, I can find out what I weighed the exact day the O.J. verdict was announced.

Does my health plan spend less money on me because I can access health care more easily? A financial assumption underlying medical homes is that people would go to the ER or let a problem fester if they didn't have such fast access to primary care, whereas I suspect that most of the time, the problem in question would simply go away on its own, like most medical issues, if someone couldn't get an instant appointment. I myself simply use more primary care when in doubt, for complaints that, as it turned out, would have self-resolved anyway during the time I would have waited to get a doctor appointment, had I not seen the doctor right away.

There is also an assumption underlying PCMH that the primary care doctor should be entrusted with managing disease because he or she is generally right about things, but that hasn't been my experience. My doctor put me on Prevacid because I got indigestion almost every night. I took Prevacid nightly for *three whole years* before I mistook a yogurt salesman in a supermarket for a store employee. After explaining that he didn't work in the store, he asked me if I ever got indigestion, and gave me a coupon for two free four-packs of Activia. Eight yogurts later, my heartburn was gone. (Just so nobody thinks I am on the payroll of Dannon, it didn't taste very good.)

Therefore, my own experience suggests that cost savings would be questionable, but this case study isn't a medical memoir—it's about claims of savings through better access to care. A cynic might say: "There already is a delivery system that delivers better access to care. It includes extended hours, extra attention for people with chronic illness, and facilitated specialist referrals. It's called *concierge medicine* and, at $4,000/year just to get started, isn't exactly a cost-savings tool."

Nonetheless, PCMH savings are claimed: Modest cost savings have been found both in severely ill populations (such as at Boeing[12]) and in integrated health care delivery settings for Medicare (such as at Geisinger[13]).

Those are special circumstances, and in any event Boeing's did not include plausibility testing. Yet, for severely ill populations and integrated delivery systems, these findings sound reasonable, even if the Boeing one was conducted by Benefits Consulting Firm A. By contrast, the study we are about to dissect, also done by Benefits Consulting Firm A, measured neither a severely ill population (only the non-disabled Medicaid population was studied in the first edition) nor an owned delivery network (the network was statewide, independent, and contracted).

The population that Benefits Consulting Firm A studied is the single broad population-based medical home study with enough data for analysis: North Carolina Medicaid. The results for North Carolina are either mind-bogglingly positive, or else someone should be going to jail. There is no in-between. As mentioned, about 37 states believe the former.

Arguably, few of these states' legislatures would have allocated money for PCMH if it hadn't been for North Carolina, which has had such a model or its precursor in place (now called Community Care of North Carolina or CCNC) for more than a decade now, showing savings now allegedly approaching $700-million/year (the state having quietly backed off previous claims of saving closer to $1 billion/year) versus the 2000 to 2002 baseline trended forward, according to the state Medicaid agency.[14]

The specific report in question here (which the earlier savings estimate is partly based on),[15] issued by Benefits Consulting Firm A and excerpted below, covered the years ending in 2006 and found "$284,000,000 to $314,000,000 in savings in 2006," versus what would have happened absent this program. One could argue that this widely accepted, often cited, outcomes report has directly or indirectly contributed to more health care policy decisions than any other single outcomes report ever. As one commentator stated: "[It's] 'the PCMH Saves Money' poster child. No presentation on the topic is complete without its mention, no Meeting Agenda is full if it's not there, if you're going to testify on the PCMH's benefits before Congress, you should bring it up, the Commonwealth Fund is working hard to replicate it and it's even embedded in Medical Home Wikipedia."[16]

Benefits Consulting Firm A's study showed more than a 12 percent reduction in overall spending versus trend. (Benefits Consulting Firm A is no stranger to validating impossible savings claims.* Recall that they also "found" 19 percent savings in a Georgia disease management program where the vendor later acknowledged they never

---

*They've also shown massive savings in many other places, too, like a Lowe's Home Improvement presentation where they showed savings in asthma up to 20 times what Lowe's *spent* on asthma events. The presentation was obviously completely wrong, but since Benefits Consulting Firm A is a competitor of mine, I kept my mouth shut (at least until afterwards, when I helped Lowe's not only to fix their error but to win an award). As John Milton said: "Never interrupt your enemy when he is making a mistake."

really got around to calling any patients.) Cited favorably by lay organizations as prestigious as NPR[17] and leading policy organizations such as the Kaiser Family Foundation,[18] all but a few states are at least considering the model partly as a result of North Carolina's success.

The savings in this Benefits Consulting Firm A report were displayed two ways: by resource (inpatient, outpatient, ER, etc.) and by age/sex category. By far the largest savings in resources was claimed in inpatient care (47 percent cost reduction representing 53 percent of overall savings). Among age/gender categories, by far the largest savings was in the 0-to-1 year M/F group (54 percent cost reduction, 50 percent of overall savings).

Note that for clarity, Tables 4.1 and 4.2 are reproduced rather than copied. Originals are available online or by contacting me.

Yet, it turns out that—if one makes the obvious assumption, articulated by another of their consulting teams, that PCMH achieves savings through utilization reduction —those two most important "findings" are totally refuted by North Carolina's own, completely publicly available, online utilization data, data which was somehow overlooked in the original analysis. Yes, the state spent millions in taxpayer money to project or estimate answers when the actual answers were available right on line the whole time.

In reality, instead of showing an average of a 47 percent reduction in inpatient utilization (almost breaking the *50 percent savings* rule on its own anyway), the utilization data shows *that no major DRG*

TABLE 4.1   Actual and Projected Use of Various Resources

Member-Months: 7,962,681

Category of Service	Projected 2006 Benchmark PMPM	Actual 2006 PMPM	Estimated Savings vs. Benchmark
Inpatient	$ 43.25	$ 23.16	$159,996,311
Outpatient	$ 23.47	$ 17.73	$ 45,660,400
Emergency Room	$ 15.11	$ 11.30	$ 303,324,253
Primary Care and Specialist	$ 56.90	$ 50.91	$ 47,751,911
Pharmacy	$ 31.72	$ 30.14	$ 12,601,550
Other	$ 30.78	$ 30.46	$ 2,516,055
Totals	$ 201.23	$ 163.70	$ 298,817,281

TABLE 4.2   Use by Age and Gender Cohort

Age and Sex Description	Member Months	Projected 2006 Benchmark PMPM	Actual 2006 PMPM	Estimated Savings vs. Benchmark
<1 year M&F	670,070	$ 411.38	$ 186.80	$ 150,479,255
1–13 years M&F	4,672,745	$ 102.70	$ 100.37	$ 10,901,303
14–18 years F	596,909	$ 224.57	$ 166.58	$ 34,614,787
14–18 years M	547,434	$ 112.82	$ 109.84	$ 1,632,831
19–44 years F	1,167,464	$ 413.89	$ 359.99	$ 62,695,031
19–44 years M	174,219	$ 452.90	$ 310.30	$ 24,844,077
> 45 years M&F	133,840	$ 665.60	$ 563.62	$ 13,949,997
Totals	**7,962,681**	**$ 201.23**	**$ 163.70**	**$ 298,817,281**

representing a significant source of inpatient care in the Medicaid population declined close to 47 percent (1) on an absolute basis; (2) versus non-Medicaid in the same state; or (3) versus Medicaid in a neighboring state. The only possible significant source of savings among 0- to 1-year-olds, neonatal utilization, declined only by about 1 percent during a period in which other states were steady, rather than the 54 percent claimed in the chart above.

For those people with altogether too much free time on their hands (in other words, people like me), this analysis is replicable through use of the Agency for Healthcare Research and Quality (AHRQ) Healthcare Cost and Utilization Project (HCUP): http://hcupnet.ahrq.gov/HCUPnet.jsp.

It looks like the most influential care management outcomes report in history is simply wrong. This report violates every rule of plausibility. As if that weren't enough, recall the time "Marvelous Marv" Throneberry hit a triple for the 1962 Mets. There was an appeals play at first base, and Throneberry was called out for failing to touch the bag. Naturally, as always happens in these circumstances, the manager, Casey Stengel, came out to argue the call. While he was arguing with the first-base umpire, the second-base umpire walked over and noted that there was no point in arguing because Throneberry hadn't touched second base, either.*

---

*Stengel, never at a loss for words, replied: "Well, I know he touched third base because he's standing on it."

In other words, if there were more rules of plausibility, this study would probably have violated them, too.

The fact that no one has publicly challenged or even closely examined these conclusions is curious given that even a cursory read of the Benefits Consulting Firm A report reveals some paradoxes, counterintuitive findings, and suspicious omissions:

1. Every element of resource use declined, a violation of the *every metric can't improve* rule. The population did not use fewer resources because it became healthier on its own. North Carolina, according to the Centers for Disease Control and Prevention, actually experienced an increase in obesity of several percentage points over this period, while diagnosed diabetes increased from roughly 7 percent to more than 9 percent over the decade, an increase comparable to most other states.[19]

2. The alleged decline in physician billings is especially counterintuitive given that primary care payments increased $2.50 to $10 per-member per-month through this model, to compensate for case management and longer hours of operation. Showing a decrease in a category that should increase is a *nexus* rule violation.

3. Inpatient expense, as mentioned, fell 47 percent. This reduction was much more than double what the AHRQ says can theoretically be saved through better care without health status improvement, since we just learned that health status deteriorated. (Not that 47 percent would have been achievable through health status improvements, either, unless they took place on a massively unprecedented scale.)

4. Expenses in the 0- to 1-year-old category fell 54 percent, even though PCMH focuses on people with chronic disease with emphasis on asthma and diabetes, two diseases rarely diagnosed in that age category, and even though:
   - Prenatal and neonatal care aren't mentioned on the CCNC home page.[20]

- The rejection of the North Carolina model by Louisiana[21] was due in large part to their inattention to high-risk pregnancy and its neonatal consequences.
- Neonates aren't generally enrolled in the state's PCMH, and therefore whatever savings they have could not be attributed to it.

5. Why did the study combine primary care and specialist visits into one category when the former is supposed to partially replace the latter?*

6. Benefits Consulting Firm A is on record as saying that "*choice* [emphasis mine] of trend has a large impact on estimates of financial savings."[22] Thus, it cannot be ruled out that Benefits Consulting Firm A's consultants, having given themselves this latitude, *chose* a trend that would allow favorable results to be shown. Otherwise, where is the insulation expense?

Those six observations by themselves do not invalidate the findings, but they do suggest that a closer look is warranted. In particular, inpatient care (#3) and infant care (#4), as noted, account for a vastly disproportionate share of savings. Fortunately, both can be analyzed using publicly available data from the federal government. We shall start with infant care for the simple reason that I didn't notice that these two vignettes were out of order until this book was out of copy-editing.

SAVINGS IN THE 0- TO 1-YEAR-OLD CATEGORY

In a voluntary program not involving economic incentives to members or employees, a 54 percent savings in *anything* should be

---

*A Freedom of Information Act request, available from the author, shows that indeed visits to both primary care physicians and specialists *per capita* increased over the period in question. However, because the thesis of this article is that one can normally draw one's own conclusions from easily available data and a critical eye, the article is not emphasizing this source of utilization increase. Additionally, the data as provided by the state seemed to be of questionable quality, so I am not relying on it and I don't know how anyone else could.

questioned—a clear violation of the *50 percent savings* rule, keeping in mind that 50 percent is a generous place to draw the line of implausibility. In this age group, the 54 percent savings can't come from pediatrician billings—their monthly capitation fee was increased. It can't come from drugs, which are not a large element of cost in this age group in the first place. In any event drug use should rise through a program in which doctors and case managers encourage compliance. It didn't come from savings through better control of childhood diseases generally—the 1- to 13-year-old category showed no savings. ER visits in this age cohort, I was told privately, fell by about 6 percent overall. Impressive totals in an absolute sense if true, but to contribute positively to an average 54 percent average cost reduction, ER visits would have to have fallen by at least 55 percent.

The only possible remaining source of savings that could exceed 54 percent is neonatal care, but as luck would have it, neonates are rarely even enrolled in the PCMH program. Nor is it clear from the state's materials that anything special was done in prenatal care during the 2000-2006 period.

Yet, because no other source could have contributed meaningfully if at all to the 54 percent average across the age category, neonatal expense would have to have fallen by vastly more than 54 percent to make up the difference. Indeed, if neonatal expenses comprise 46 percent or less of all expenses in that age group, they would need to be reduced by more than the *100 percent* rule would allow, in order to generate average savings for that age cohort of 54 percent. Even so, a simple analysis of the HCUP DRGs for North Carolina, reproduced below, shows that neonatal discharges and days of care *increased* over that period on an absolute basis, and decreased only slightly as a percentage of all birth events.

The result from that database follows. The discharges and days for neonates are compared to the discharges and days for normal deliveries. The three years of baseline (2000 to 2002) are contrasted to the study year, 2006. The line in bold italics shows that neonatal utilization fell by 1 percent, not 100 percent, over that period—a mistake of two orders of magnitude. (The state and their consultants would no doubt argue that neonatal discharge rates would have risen dramatically over that period without the PCMH, but a similar analysis for South Carolina shows that—even absent a PCMH—that state's neonatal discharge rate fell by almost the same amount over the same period.)

Discharges (DRGs)	Baseline Study 2000–2002	Baseline Study 2006
Non-normal (386–390)	30,545	32,390
Normal (391)	111,006	122,033
% of Total Non-Normal Discharges	**27.5%**	**26.5%**

Conclusion: there was no significant savings in the neonatal population, versus the decrease of probably more than 100 percent needed to create the average savings across the age category of 54 percent. Hence, "invalidated" is a nice word for what happened to the 54 percent savings claim. ("Eviscerated" is more appropriate.) And as mentioned, there was no prenatal or neonatal intervention anyway.

Once again, Benefits Consulting Firm A found savings of greater than 100 percent in a category in which there could not have been any savings at all because nothing was done. With respect to impossible outcomes, Benefits Consulting Firm A is truly the consulting industry's Will Rogers. (Google it.)

INPATIENT CARE GENERALLY

The AHRQ HCUP database captures all DRGs that comprise all inpatient admissions, by payer, by state. Therefore, it is easy enough for anyone to see which DRGs fell 47 percent in North Carolina Medicaid. Medicaid has, as compared to the commercially insured population, a disproportionate share of admissions not just in birth events (which as we just noted barely fell), but also in asthma, a disease category in which Medicaid recipients usually comprise the majority of a state's hospital admissions.

In addition to its prevalence, asthma is an excellent choice to test the 47 percent savings hypothesis for two other reasons as well:

1. It is one of the AHRQ's Ambulatory Care-Sensitive Conditions (ACSC), meaning that it has been independently determined that good ambulatory care can make a noticeable difference in the need for hospitalizations for asthma.
2. The CCNC program's home page places a special emphasis on asthma prevention—justifiably so, considering its combination of prevalence and avoidable admissions.

Therefore, if *any* category of admissions would be expected to exceed the 47 percent average savings across all DRGS that was claimed by Benefits Consulting Firm A, it would be asthma. Indeed, the HCUP database reveals a decline in the admission rate for North Carolina Medicaid for the three asthma DRGs in use at the time (DRGs 96 through 98) of 21 percent, from 2001 to 2006. That by itself, of course, is far less than the claimed average of 47 percent savings, and—while impressive *prima facie* in an absolute sense, asthma savings should be pulling the 47 percent average up. If asthma didn't decline more than 47 percent, what did?

And *prima facie* impressiveness means just that—impressive on its face. If we go deeper, even that result has a Toto issue. It turns out that the asthma admission rate in North Carolina's *non-Medicaid* population fell almost as much as the Medicaid population. Depending on whether one counts the rest of the state's commercially insured or the neighboring state's Medicaid population as the "usual care" control group, asthma fell either 4 percent or 17.3 percent. Impressive performances but not close to 47 percent in the category in which the greatest declines would be expected.

Discrete Population	Decline in Asthma DRG Admissions during First Study Period (2000/2 to 2006)
North Carolina Medicaid	−34.8%
North Carolina Non-Medicaid	−30.8%
South Carolina Medicaid	−17.5%

Diabetes is another category of care specifically highlighted on the CCNC home page as a focus of prevention.[23] Yet, diabetes admissions (DRG 294 and 295) showed a *negative* performance difference versus non-Medicaid and versus South Carolina. Due to the increased prevalence of diabetes, all three cohorts increased, but North Carolina Medicaid increased at a rate double that of non-Medicaid and four times that of South Carolina Medicaid.

Discrete Population	Increase in Diabetes DRG Admissions during First Study Period (2000/2 to 2006)
North Carolina Medicaid	+10.2%
North Carolina Non-Medicaid	+4.1%
South Carolina Medicaid	+2.6%

Netted out against each other, there were basically no savings in the two disease categories most likely *a priori* to show savings. A scan of every other major DRG in the HCUP data set found no DRG accounting for greater than 1,000 discharges declining more than 47 percent as compared to the non-Medicaid population. Most had no significant decline at all, versus the non-Medicaid population.

A Top-Down Confirmation

The Benefits Consulting Firm A analysis—and my smackdown of it—has been what one might refer to as a *bottoms-up* analysis, looking at individual admissions categories and then summing them up and finding large gaps. One always tries to confirm analyses using completely different approaches, in this case a top-down analysis in which total hospital admissions are compared.

In 2011, the federal government's Medicaid and CHIP Payment Access Commission published a comparison of Medicaid spending levels by state in www.macpac.gov/reports.

Of the three major age categories, the North Carolina PCMH until recently applied to two: children and adults up to 64 years old. Adults 65 and over comprise the "aged" category in Medicaid. The PCMH does not apply to the aged category because Medicare, not Medicaid, is the primary payor for medical expenses, while the large majority of Medicaid spending is on nursing homes.

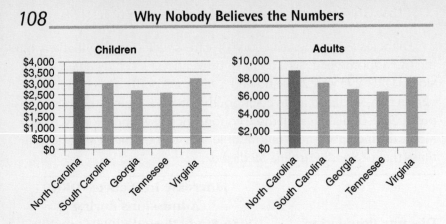

FIGURE 4.8 Comparison of Per Capita Medicaid Spending, Children and Adults, North Carolina versus Surrounding States

If the North Carolina PCMH saved the $681 million dollars a year that they say it does now, you would expect that the state's ranking for *per capita* spending would be lower than surrounding states for children and adults. Instead, it's the highest in both age groupings (Figure 4.8).

The other explanation is that North Carolina is simply a higher-cost place to do Medicaid business than surrounding states, and/or offers a richer benefit. Therefore, even with all the savings, North Carolina would still be a high-cost state. If that were the case one would expect the aged category to be high-cost too because (1) this is still North Carolina we're looking at and last we checked two sentences ago, it was high-cost and (2) the savings available from PCMH barely reaches the aged population, whose primary payor is Medicare, so if anything the aged should be *higher*-cost. However, it turns out that just the opposite is true—NC is the *lowest-cost* state for the aged as shown in Figure 4.9.

Nor is it the case that medical insurance generally is more expensive in North Carolina than elsewhere. It appears to be about average for the region.[24] Nope—looks like the only outsized expense in North Carolina is its PCMH-infused Medicaid population.

BUT WAIT—THERE'S MORE. NOW HOW MUCH WOULD YOU PAY?

The North Carolina infomercial for PCMH has expanded since the Benefits Consulting Firm A study. Consulting Company B alleged that

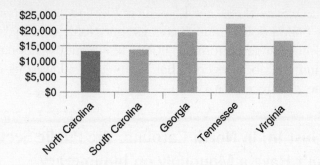

FIGURE 4.9 Per Capita Spending on the Aged

the North Carolina savings through 2009 tripled since 2006. Just from 2007 to 2008, they conjured up savings almost equivalent to what Benefits Consulting Firm A said North Carolina saved from 2000 to 2006. Unfortunately, neither admissions nor ER visits declined between 2007 and 2008. North Carolina, apparently unsatisfied with Benefits Consulting Firm A's previous fiction, layered on top of it Consulting Company B's pure fantasy.

Putting both studies together, the annual savings rate versus the baseline-adjusted-for-trend would be approaching a billion dollars (a total of $1.5 billion over 2007 – 2009) despite an admission rate trend that looked like this Figure 4.10.

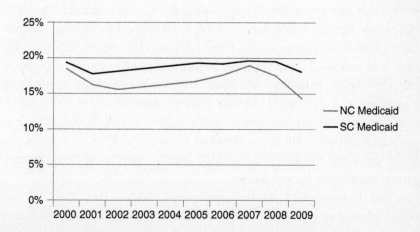

FIGURE 4.10 Admission Rates for North Carolina versus South Carolina

Not only was there no 47 percent decline in admissions, or therefore billion-dollar annual savings, but North Carolina's admissions decline underperformed PCMH-less South Carolina. (Both states—and just about every other state—saw admissions declines during the 2009 recession.)

This Just In: In North Carolina, the Public Sector Doesn't Have a Monopoly on Innumeracy

Apparently, Blue Cross of North Carolina likes what it sees in Medicaid. According to a press release published as *Why Nobody Believes* was going to press,[25] it is joining Medicaid in its medical home model, and touting the findings from the Consulting Company B analysis as the basis for its decision:

"CCNC is known for providing the state's Medicaid program with 'on the ground' care management, health information technology infrastructure and population-based health initiatives that have raised quality and saved Medicaid nearly $1.5 billion over three years."

OOPS! THEY DID IT AGAIN

Also as *Why Nobody Believes* was going to press, yet another actuarial study, this one from Consulting Company C, was released. The only difference between this one—which showed somewhat less savings than Consulting Company B's showed—and the others was that this one was released nine months behind schedule, perhaps because the Outcomes Fairy had so many other commitments. Consulting Company C's estimated annual savings rate in 2009 vs. a 2006 baseline is $382 million, presumably added to the $299 million in savings through 2006 from Benefits Consulting Firm A's study. So these guys are showing "only" $681 million in total annual savings, rather than close to $1 billion.

You'd think with all that time and money the study would have refuted or at least acknowledged the two federal databases showing exactly the opposite of their conclusions. But it appears that these guys also never even *found* those two databases. (Not finding the HCUP database appears to be a prerequisite for being hired to consult for North Carolina.) Or perhaps Consulting Company C subcontracted this work to their Beijing office, which didn't have access to Google. Either that or they suppressed the findings that didn't agree with their conclusions. But no researcher would ever do that. Would they?

To answer the other obvious questions: No, they never checked the actual nexus between the intervention and the sources of utilization reduction, meaning they didn't check, for example, diabetes or asthma admissions. Instead they guessed at the reasons for the alleged savings. No, they didn't compare North Carolina to South Carolina or any other state Medicaid program, which means that, no, they didn't explain away the increase in admissions relative to South Carolina. No, they didn't see if PCP visits rose relative to specialist visits or if fewer high-cost diagnostic tests were done or if fewer people visited the emergency room. No, they didn't do any population-based plausibility testing whatsoever. And, no, they don't claim any facility in analysis of care management outcomes (as I likewise would never claim facility in matters actuarial) or even attempt any such analysis. Instead they call it "very difficult." They were wrong about that too. An analysis is quite easy if the answers are already available online.

What they did do were all sorts of machinations at taxpayer expense, splitting up the population into those who were in the program (most of them) and those who weren't (a few of them) and assign all sorts of assumptions for risk scores, trend, health status differences between the groups, amount of time in the program, and length of continuous enrollment, and lots of pre-post stuff.

They basically did every possible analysis of a state whose savings are driven by utilization changes in the population as a whole, except for analyzing the utilization of the population as a whole. And they analyzed all the possible data, except for the data made freely available by the federal government for the very purpose of doing this type of analysis.

Had they decided instead to actually look at the data and answer the question: "Did the state's utilization decline through this statewide program?" instead of lamenting about how very difficult it is, below is what they would have found. Once again, in the benefit-of-the-doubt department, we'll consider utilization only in the two "canary in the coal mine" categories most likely to show reduction, asthma and diabetes, and use the same analysis as before. We are focusing on relative rather than absolute changes both because (1) the DRGs changed in 2008 and because (2) changes in prevalence and usual care would occur in all three populations over a decade. A brief note for the literal-minded: The study went through fiscal 2010, which would include the second half of 2009. My data ends in December 2009 for now. So the periods aren't identical but the results are far enough off what would be needed to support the Consulting Company C conclusions that six months wouldn't matter.

Discrete Asthma Population	Change in Asthma DRG Admissions during Second Study Period (2006 to 2009)
North Carolina Medicaid	+8.0%
North Carolina Non-Medicaid	−24.5%
South Carolina Medicaid	−17.8%

Discrete Population	Change in Diabetes DRG Admissions during Second Study Period (2006 to 2009)
North Carolina Medicaid	−2.1%
North Carolina Non-Medicaid	−9.8%
South Carolina Medicaid	−0.1%

Let's put the whole shebang together to see what happened over the course of the entire decade.

Discrete Population	Change in Asthma DRG Admissions during First Study Period (2000/2 to 2006)	Change in Asthma DRG Admissions during Second Study Period (2006 to 2009)	*Total Change in Asthma Admissions, 2000/2 to 2009*
North Carolina Medicaid	−34.8%	+8.0%	*−29.5%*
North Carolina Non-Medicaid	−30.8%	−24.5%	*−32.2%*
South Carolina Medicaid	−17.5%	−17.8%	*−47.7%*

Discrete Population	Change in Diabetes DRG Admissions during First Study Period (2000/2 to 2006)	Change in Diabetes DRG Admissions during Second Study Period (2006 to 2009)	Total Change in Diabetes Admissions, 2000/2 to 2009
North Carolina Medicaid	+10.2%	−2.1%	*+7.9%*
North Carolina Non-Medicaid	+4.1%	−0.1%	*+3.9%*
South Carolina Medicaid	+2.6%	−9.8%	*−7.4%*

In both the conditions, which received the most emphasis by CCNC, the admission rate for Medicaid underperformed both reference groups, North Carolina non-Medicaid and South Carolina Medicaid. This analysis could be recreated for other DRGs,* but there is no reason to think that the conditions that weren't emphasized in CCNC would outperform the ones that were emphasized in the

---

*I did, and most other DRGs show the same thing.

program, and in any event as noted earlier, the entire North Carolina Medicaid admissions rate underperformed South Carolina Medicaid.

Breaking News: Consulting Company C's Pants Are on Fire

I don't know why I didn't uncover this earlier (my only excuse being that no one else uncovered it at all), but I just noticed, after having written the entire book and even sent it to copy-editing, that Consulting Company C simply made up its savings figures. They claimed about $250,000,000 in savings in children's inpatient admissions, but HCUP says the state only *had* $114,000,000 in those admissions during the baseline year of 2006, so it would have been impossible to save $250,000,000 in 2009. Not that it matters, because as it turns out, the children's admission rate actually *increased*, relative to neighboring states, over the 2006-2009 period. So most of their alleged savings, along with all of their credibility, are wiped out even without all the other observations in this chapter.

The good news is the report does contain one true conclusion: "Other [Company C] consultants may hold different views." See Figure 4.11.

Consulting Company C will likely object to this analysis using some actuarial double-speak about risk adjustments, trend, pre-post study design, and how very difficult this analysis is, but since they suppressed, ignored, or overlooked this HCUP and relative-cost data earlier, they really aren't in any position to turn around and whine about it now. The bottom line is, the financial justification of a statewide Medicaid PCMH is mostly based on reducing population-wide inpatient admissions, and this one didn't.

CONCLUSION AND LESSONS FOR POLICYMAKERS

At this point it would be easier to conclude that North Carolina lost money (because it increased fees paid to physicians) than that the state saved $300 million in 2006 alone, let alone a run rate of either

North Carolina Division of Medical Assistance
Estimated Cost Savings Calculated Using Method 1 by Fiscal Year and Eligibility Group

Fiscal Year	ABD Medicaid Only	ABD Dual Eligibles	Children age 20 and under (excluding ABD)	Adults (excluding ABD)	Totals
FY07	($82,000,000)	($14,000,000)	$177,000,000	$22,000,000	$103,000,000
FY08	($34,000,000)	($9,000,000)	$202,000,000	$45,000,000	$204,000,000
FY09	($13,000,000)	($11,000,000)	$261,000,000	$58,000,000	$295,000,000
FY10	($53,000,000)	($6,000,000)	$238,000,000	$97,000,000	$382,000,000

Aggregate costs		of Discharges	Medicare	Medicaid
Total number of discharges		1,105,005	423,602	226,190
		########	########	########
Age group	<1	136,849	19	69,019
		390,703,783	6,228	227,790,451
	17-Jan	44,546	11	22,394
		250,617,666	365,929	114,620,426
		289,755	21,669	97,859
		########	178,553,996	487,584,960
	45-64	265,992	72,447	36,442
		########	729,137,435	369,788,731
	65-84	299,251	264,785	429
		########	########	4,874,779
	85+	69,595	64,563	39
		531,179,285	495,677,349	335,288

2006 baseline spending On Medicaid children's admissions

FIGURE 4.11 Comparison of Savings Plan from Milliman Report to HCUP-Reported Hospital Cost.

$681 million or almost $1 billion/year today, depending on which study(ies) you want to believe. We can't rule out small savings in emergency room visits (except in the only years we have data for, 2008 and 2009, where there were none) and other expenses that are not easily checked via public data, but by far the two largest sources of claimed savings through 2006, infants and inpatient care, turn out to show very minor savings and increased utilization, respectively, while physician expenses rose because PMPM fees were increased. And most of their savings since 2006 proved mathematically impossible too. The bottom line: the whole thing was made up.

Further, the comparative cost data indicates exactly what the *Why Nobody Believes* analysis indicates: Extra expenses for PCMH may have turned North Carolina into a high-cost state for Medicaid.

How such an obviously incorrect cost savings figure could have been accepted by the state is understandable. The same Medicaid administrators who put the PCMH program in place hired their own consultants to validate it, and the majority of North Carolina's Medicaid expenses are federally financed anyway, so a finding of savings leading to more funding was a financial and political gain for the state. A state presentation to the legislature highlighted exactly that— the availability of generous federal funding to continue and expand the program.

For its part, Benefits Consulting Firm A received tremendous positive publicity for this finding, and has done more business with the state's Medicaid program since then. Further, it is likely that most North Carolina administrators backed the program in the first place because they believed, probably justifiably based on my own experience that a PCMH program would increase access and quality, and these positive feelings may easily have influenced the objectivity of the study sponsors.

What is much more puzzling is, how could the rest of the country's policymakers (and North Carolina Blue Cross) have so willingly accepted this result (in the case of Blue Cross, even quoting Consulting Company B's findings, findings that Medicaid itself has quietly backed off), when an hour online refutes everything conclusively? Even without checking the data online, the plausibility rules can provide some lessons for policymakers reading outcomes studies:

1. Large savings claims in voluntary programs are usually invalid.
2. Everything can't decline because people have to be getting their care from somewhere.
3. A program focused in one area (in this case chronic disease) can't be getting most of its savings from another area untouched by the program (infants).
4. Consider the incentives of the people doing the study before accepting their findings* (not technically a plausibility rule but a good rule in life, and an especially good rule, as we will see, when reading a Health Plan H study).

---

*The best example of this is the Health Plan H study we are about to deconstruct, in which a group of Health Plan H clinical pharmacists found that using clinical pharmacists at Health Plan H would yield a 57:1 ROI and reduce the death rate of cardiac patients due to non-cardiac causes by 90 percent.

Population health improvement studies, in which cost savings are "soft" and assumption-influenced, are especially susceptible to invalid conclusions. There are no standards and no double-blind trials for care management outcomes reporting, and only one training/certification program in care management outcomes evaluation.[26] There is, however, critical thinking. A larger emphasis on that would do more than any government program or payment mechanism innovation to control the cost of health care.

In addition to the general lesson about the importance of the plausibility rules, there are two specific policy lessons. One is at the state level: Medicaid agencies shouldn't be giving up the managed care model in favor of the medical home model yet. The former is budgetable and the savings are clear, whereas the latter involves an immediate increase in payments to primary care providers with no clear offset in reduced inpatient utilization.

The other is at the federal level: Either switch to block grants and let the states make mistakes with no federal matching funds consequences, or require that all programs requiring federal matching funds be evaluated by disinterested federally financed evaluators, rather than by taxpayer-financed consultants, chosen by the state, who prefer to concoct their own answers rather than simply google the correct ones.

Case Study #3: Are Health Plan H's Doctors Killing Their Patients?

Health Plan H reported that their cardiac care intervention saved $21,000/patient/year through more aggressive and earlier use of cardiac drugs post-heart attack, through a program supervised by Health Plan H's pharmacists being billed at only $361.25/patient-year.[27] This study, which I would encourage you to have handy as you read this chapter, combines violations of several existing plausibility rules and, like the Benefits Consulting Firm A study, suggests that if we had more plausibility rules, they would have violated those too.

For instance, drug costs *fell* roughly 20 percent for the intervention group relative to the control group, despite the authors' assertions that "early initiation of secondary preventive drug therapy" and "aggressive use of secondary prevention drugs" were largely responsible for the outcomes improvement in the intervention group. This is a violation of the *quality dose–cost response* rule: If drug use falls, then obviously drugs were not used aggressively. (It's also a violation of a rule that says a journal should find peer reviewers who are actually going to read, and possibly even understand, the article they are reviewing.)

It is highly implausible *either* that a larger, earlier dosage of the appropriate drugs could cost less than a smaller, later dosage of the inappropriate ones, *or* that a clinical pharmacist being resourced at less than \$1/patient/day was able to identify appropriate drug therapy far more effectively than the physicians for Health Plan H's control group. However, *both* statements must be true for the outcome to be real.

More concerning from a quality perspective than the *quality dose–cost response* rule violation is the magnitudinal difference in the death rates between the two groups. Almost one-third of the matched control group (you guessed it—"matched controls" are a *control group equivalency* rule violation) died, as opposed to 2.6 percent of the study group.

And yet, despite this life-saving effectiveness, Health Plan H elected not to make this \$1/day intervention the standard of care. It's not like this would have required a financial sacrifice: \$21,000 in annual savings/patient versus costs of \$361.25 yields a THC-induced ROI of 57:1, an ROI at least a magnitude higher than any other ROI not calculated by Benefits Consulting Firm A* ever formally reported in disease management. If the study is to be believed, failing to institutionalize that standard of care cost Health Plan H \$21,000/patient in annualized savings, an amount in excess of what a typical cardiac patient costs a typical health plan in total.

A violation of the *nexus* rule is in the non-cardiac death rate. This was an intervention on cardiac patients in which the cardiac drug

---

*In the aforementioned North Carolina study, Benefits Consulting Firm A found a 24:1 ROI in the first full year alone. In the immortal words of the great philosopher Sammy Davis Jr., nice work if you can get it.

regimen was changed by Health Plan H's Collaborative Cardiac Care Service. Yet, the reduction in the death rate in the intervention group due to non-cardiac causes was three times that of the reduction in the death rate due to the cardiac causes that the intervention was specifically designed to reduce.

Furthermore, if the study is to be believed, the control group's doctors were guilty of almost criminal negligence. It wasn't just that the control group died at a rate ten times that of the allegedly equivalent study group. What makes it negligent is that one must conclude that the death rate differential was due to the control group's doctors' *prima facie* failure to adequately medicate the control group, because drug spend accounted for only slightly more than 2 percent of the $93,800 in total annualized spending per person. Two percent is roughly *one-tenth* of the average percentage of claims devoted to drugs for the average health plan member, yet these members were thirty times sicker than the average health plan member and ten times sicker than the intervention group, as measured by their relative death rates. Indeed in absolute dollars, the drug spend in the control group was far below the average for the U.S. population in the control group's age category.

Also, the more the patients went to the doctor, the more likely they were to die—the study group had about 12 percent fewer doctor visits than the control group. With robust declines in drug spend, pharmacy, and physician expense, this study violates the *every metric can't improve* rule.

To summarize: If the study was valid, the following are all true:

1. Health Plan H's doctors were negligent.
2. Health Plan H's executives ignored $21,000 in savings per patient.
3. Health Plan H's clinical pharmacists (who were the clinical investigators for the study) performed brilliantly, dramatically improving outcomes and reducing the non-cardiac death rate through a cardiac intervention, while significantly reducing drug costs, all for $1/patient/day.

More than likely, however, the control group's doctors were adhering to the standard of care, Health Plan H's executives were acting responsibly, and the incongruous published outcome is instead due to innumeracy or a hidden agenda, such as – just a wild-posterior guess here – a group of clinical pharmacists authoring a study to "prove" the value of clinical pharmacy consults in order to get reimbursed for them. A much more likely explanation for the result is that lack of a governing body, formal rules, or understanding of plausibility allowed this study to pass internal review by Health Plan H and external peer review by *Pharmacotherapy*.

There aren't plausibility rules for every contingency, but if there were, another rule would be that a study flunks plausibility if it ignores or suppresses highly counterintuitive findings. In this case, among other things they didn't explain:

- Why drug use was so low in general and even lower in the study group.
- Why cardiac patients cost Health Plan H $90,000/year instead of $20,000/year like every other health plan, making it possible to save $21,000/patient.
- Why the *non-cardiac* death rate was 22 times higher in the control group versus the study group (as compared to a cardiac death rate at about 8 times higher) even though this is a "collaborative cardiac care service" focused on cardiac pharmacotherapy.
- Why the 57:1 ROI was deemed too unimportant to mention.
- Why the ROI was magnitudinally higher than what other care management programs achieve.

Case Study #4: Vendor A Cures Health Plan I's CHF Patients

We mentioned Vendor A in the introduction as an example of epidemiologically impossible results. Here is Exhibit A to that effect.

The only problem with this Vendor A study is that it violates so many of the plausibility rules that I almost don't know what category to fit it in. So, I'll be making reference to many of the rules, while focusing on the *50 percent savings* rule. In fact, with the possible exception of North Carolina Medicaid, no one violates as many rules to as large a degree as Vendor A. Hence, the *multiple violations* rule.

Vendor A's study using Health Plan I's Medicare patients starts with a violation of the *50 percent savings* rule, as the following graphic is shown in support of Vendor A's claim that admission rates for heart failure patients fell 79 percent, essentially from the start of their telephone support program (the *quality dose–cost response* rule violation—it should have taken much longer) from 1,636 admissions per 1,000 patients to 351 admissions/1,000 patients. Their case study also claims an 85 percent reduction in overall costs, which violates the *every metric can't improve* rule, since non-admissions costs had to be falling much more than admissions rates in order for a 79 percent admissions decline to translate into an 85 percent cost savings. To reduce all costs by more than 85 percent, they would have to cure CHF without incurring costs to do so, sort of like the way the immortal philosopher ET cured the boo-boo on Eliot's finger.

The following chart is an approximation of the chart now removed from their website. Funny thing—Vendor A sent around an email urging people to share these results with the world, but when I offered to share them with the world, they denied me permission. So my reproduction (Figure 4.12) on page 122 may be a tiny bit off.

No peer-reviewed result has ever shown a 79 percent decline in all-cause admissions for heart failure, triggering an 85 percent overall cost reduction. Historically, most studies on heart failure have shown a much lower reduction of admissions. Cross-sectional, mostly unpublished, data from health plans with heart failure disease management programs generally shows roughly a 2 to 5 percent reduction per year in heart failure-specific admissions with a disease management program in place. Generating all-cause admission reduction is a far more difficult feat than generating admission reduction specifically for heart failure fluid overload, because the former requires avoiding admissions unrelated to CHF. While a similar analysis for CHF has never been undertaken, the American Diabetes Association found that 63 percent of admissions for diabetics are for diagnoses not specifically related to diabetes.[28]

With that study as background, it is hard to imagine how directed self-monitoring could reduce overall admissions for CHF patients—including admissions not specifically related to CHF such as elective surgeries, trauma, and cancer—by 79 percent when most other

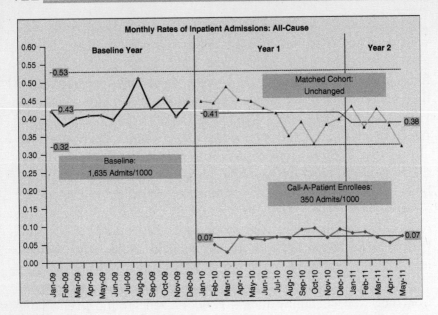

FIGURE 4.12   The Largest Utilization Reduction Claim in Disease Management History

programs generate only a 2 to 5 percent reduction in admissions related closely to CHF.

One could also make a case for a *100 percent* rule violation. Certainly CHF admissions avoidable through phone calls and monitoring, such as fluid overload, are less costly than admissions not avoidable through phone calls, such as falls, cancer, and transplants. Suppose one replaces the implicit assumption that a 79 percent reduction in admissions generates a 79 percent reduction in hospital costs with a more realistic assumption that a 79 percent reduction in admissions reduces hospital costs by somewhat less than 79 percent, due to the lower acuity of admissions actually avoided (like fluid overload), as compared to unavoidable admissions (like transplants). In that case, non-hospital costs would have to fall by quite a bit more, likely more than 100 percent, to generate an 85 percent overall savings.

There are other issues with this study, as well. Yes, you guessed correctly: Only active volunteer enrollees are measured, not the entire study group. Hence motivation is required to get into the intervention group for rather than be equally distributed across the two groups—exactly the opposite of what biostatisticians would recommend and a violation of the *control group equivalency* rule.

And the *matched control* is simply a set of people who had the same risk scores in the study year that the intervention group had in the baseline, before the latter regressed to the mean, and before about half of the latter self-selected into the program. The matched control is also a lesson in the Power of Positive Thinking. It is labeled as "unchanged" but look again: the "unchanged" group declined about 25%.

Two other curiosities worth noting:

1. Vendor A cited a "strong enrollment rate" as one of the reasons this program was successful in reducing costs and admissions. Yet, even as the enrollment rate climbed (meaning, improved) about 30 percent over the course of the study, the admission rate *increased* (meaning, got worse) by roughly the same amount. Admissions therefore correlated inversely, not directly, with the enrollment rate. The data would, then, appear to show exactly the opposite of the statement that a "strong enrollment rate" was responsible for the study's success.

2. Whereas in most disease management programs, improvements take place gradually, as members are re-educated and brought under control, here the most dramatic admissions reductions, almost 90 percent, took place in the first two reported months, starting only four weeks after program initiation, as stated earlier a violation of the *quality dose–cost response* rule.

There were two other smoking guns that invalidate this Vendor A study. First, Health Plan I requested that Vendor A remove the study from their website, following my observations. Second soon thereafter, the *New England Journal of Medicine* published a result based on a Vendor A intervention showing neither admissions reductions nor savings.[29]

Now you see why we have a *multiple violations* rule. It's tough to violate one rule without violating a ton of others along the way.

Keep those cards and letters coming in, folks

I wouldn't have all these Case Studies in Cluelessness Gone Wild if people didn't send them to me. They are catalogued on my website, www.dismgmt.com, under Intelligent Design Awards, lovingly bestowed on companies that set back the evolution of the health management field. Feel free to suggest others.

Chapter 5

Case Studies of Where, When, and How Wellness Programs Have Actually Worked

You weren't expecting this chapter, were you?

But there are some situations—in wellness, disease management, and coordinated care—where good results have been very well documented. (For patient-centered medical homes, the jury is still out on actual savings. But based on the evidence so far, if I were the plaintiff I'd be looking to cop a plea.) The odd thing is, these positive results rarely come from conventional programs, involving a lot of nurses, coaches, surveys, and telephones. These next three chapters will offer examples. Since I don't want to leave anyone out, if you have examples of programs that work, send them in and I will highlight them on my website, to contrast them to the plethora of programs that don't work.

This chapter will provide two examples from wellness that are diametric opposites. One does what most of the Case Studies in Cluelessness Gone Wild claim they did: Take steps to make an older workforce healthier.

The other does exactly the opposite: It gradually replaces an unhealthy workforce with a healthier one.

What neither does is what the case study vendors say they do: save gazillions of dollars right away, almost as soon as people complete their HRAs (if not beforehand, in the case of Vendor M). Think about it: If you completed an HRA what could you possibly learn about yourself that you don't already know that could cause your medical costs to decline within months? Or as I sometimes say when I present publicly: "Raise your hand if you smoke and don't realize you should quit."

Quite the opposite: The Highmark study teaches that, as in anything else, you have to invest money to save money, and that's what this first study shows.

Case Study #1: Encouraging Health Prevention—at a Cost

Anyone who likes irony will appreciate this next example. You recall those Case Studies in Cluelessness Gone Wild announcing impossible savings, never plausibility-checked, that come from some black box methodology, even making up terms like "undetected claims cost"? Turns out that the only example of transparent impact of wellness that we could find in the whole wellness industry—the only case that satisfies a plausibility test—comes from a company actually *named* Black Box.

You might ask: "Wait a second. Aren't there plenty of examples in the literature of companies that saved money on wellness?"

You are half right.

There are indeed plenty of examples in the literature of companies that *say* they saved money in wellness. But the results are never plausibility-tested. It's always: "We put in a program and our costs went down." No study ever tests whether the change was due to the program. No study (including the otherwise industry-best Highmark study cited in this book, where costs initially increased) asks: "Yes, but did the utilization of medical services decline in the categories in which one would expect utilization to decline, having first increased in the categories where utilization would be expected to increase in advance of that decrease?"

And: "Was it across the entire population rather than just for participants?"

No one, anywhere, addresses those questions in print—until now. Like Diogenes, I've been searching for an honest outcome, with a lantern powered by plausibility.

In this example—just like in the Highmark study—an emphasis on wellness has initially caused costs to increase. But the costs that have increased at Black Box, as you'll see, are "good" medical costs, oriented to prevention. The important thing is the needle was actually moved. That by itself is a rarity.

A bit of background on Black Box: Black Box is a global, 4,000-employee company specializing in communication solutions for complex voice and data networks. Several divisions have the same health benefit and hence are exposed to the same plan design changes over time, thus holding that variable constant. Of the four divisions for which data is available, one—imaginatively referred to here as Division A—actively began pursuing a wellness program in 2008, but didn't move any needles. Low participation increased only modestly until they switched vendors starting in 2010. The analysis focuses on what has happened in Division A compared to three other divisions, collectively referred to hereafter as Division BCD. Additionally, Division A's wellness program focused only on employees, so preventive care would be expected to increase for employees only, not spouses.

That means there are really two sets of controls: (1) Divisions BCD versus A and (2) employees versus spouses.

In 2008, Division A began their wellness initiatives with their first wellness partner, a regional Midwest vendor. The program consisted of the standard-issue vanilla wellness activities—biometric testing, voluntary health coaching, health risk assessments, and quarterly wellness challenges. The Year One award was a $25 gift certificate. In Year 2, up to $1,000 could be earned, based on the number of program offerings an employee completed. Culture and communications lagged though, and even with $1,000 on the table, participation reached only 40 percent.

That was probably just as well. It would be tough to save anything remotely close to $1,000 per employee through a wellness program, even measuring absenteeism and presenteeism.

In 2010, Division A replaced the incumbent and introduced a revamped program with a new vendor/partner. After an employee survey revealed how highly members valued their relationship with their physician, the program was redesigned to emphasize a preventive visit with one's physician following the HRA. The reward was a 15 percent reduction in employee-paid premiums for participants who met all the requirements.

Even though this reward fell far short of the $1,000 offered in conjunction with the previous program, the first year with the new vendor saw an increase in HRA completion from 39 percent to 73 percent, while over 60 percent of U.S. employees met all requirements and hence earned their premium reduction. As of this writing, the momentum appears to have clearly continued through 2011, though all the results won't be known until after *Why Nobody Believes* is published.

The common thread over the past four years has been Alan Perry, human resources vice president, and his vision to positively influence individual accountability for personal health. With strong executive support from Black Box CFO Mike McAndrew, Director of Finance Tim Huffmyer, and the diligent efforts of Perry's human resources team, the vision is becoming a reality. Preventive visits with primary providers or active participation in behavior-modifying lifestyle risk programs were the identified behaviors to target. First-year success was defined as getting this culture of prevention in motion. The Black Box team identified physician visits, screening tests, and possibly ER visits as near-term outcomes metrics to monitor the impact of their wellness efforts, with specific inpatient event and procedure reduction to be tracked in later years.

The following two tables compare the results of cholesterol screening and wellness visits for employees, men and women separately, over 40 years of age. The rates for Division A male and female employees who were exposed to wellness program expectations and messaging about the value of preventive visits and biometric screening are significantly higher than Division BCD.

Category and Gender	Division A	Divisions BCD	Difference
Male Employees			
Cholesterol Screening	57%	46%	*24%*
Preventive Visits	35%	20%	*75%*
Female Employees			
Cholesterol Screening	51%	36%	*42%*
Preventive Visits	62%	39%	*59%*

Of course, women had more visits, women being considered the more conscientious of the two genders with respect to getting preventive medical care, as well as with respect to pretty much everything else except perhaps ensuring an adequate supply of beer on Super Sunday (and even so I'd still give the nod to women if that calculation includes light beer). However, the males improved at a greater rate and also did get more blood lipid testing, which is a good thing because in the 40- to 65-year-old cohort, heart events are more common in males than females.

The other control was the difference—a large gap—between employees and non-employee spouses, who were not included in the program in 2010:

2010 Preventive Visits

Category and Gender	Employees	Spouses	Difference
Males			
Division A	35%	15%	*127%*
Divisions BCD	20%	15%	*33%*
Females			
Division A	62%	49%	*27%*
Divisions BCD	39%	45%	*−13%*

2010 Cholesterol Screening

Category and Gender	Employees	Spouses	Difference
Males			
Division A	57%	38%	*50%*
Divisions BCD	46%	38%	*21%*
Females			
Division A	51%	36%	*42%*
Divisions BCD	36%	34%	*6%*

Note that, as in Highmark, initial success means higher cost. Changing one's health status is a long-term or at least intermediate-term endeavor. The leading consultants in this industry—defined as the two who have managed to get certified in Critical Outcomes Report Analysis (CORA)—would agree. Melissa Tobler, who consults to Black Box, says: "The plausibility indicators for the early stages of a wellness program, screenings and doctor visits, typically carry higher costs, offset by a possible decline in ER visits. But those costs are investments in preventive health that will pay off over time in reduced medical events, bariatric surgeries, smoking-related illness and even diagnoses of new cases of diabetes, metabolic syndrome, and CAD."

Dave Rearick, DO, the other consultant who has achieved CORA Certification, agrees: "It boggles the mind that vendors still race to outdo one another's high short-term ROI claims with even higher and shorter-term ROI claims, when at this point any sophisticated buyer knows there is no short-term ROI from wellness, high or otherwise."

Still, there seem to be enough of what Christopher Robin might call "consultants of very little brain" to enable the robust growth of vendors promising almost immediate ROIs.

Case Study #2: Do You Really Want to Create a Culture of Wellness? Are You Sure?

Before you start taking furious notes here, keep in mind that a "culture of wellness" is not automatically a good idea. True, the more you push to create this culture, the more your health status will improve, the more your medical claims will fall ... and possibly the worse off you will be. Remember, you are not in business to reduce your healthcare costs. You are in business to make money, which requires being able to attract and retain the best employees, and motivate them to do their best work.* To use an extreme

---

*Creating this culture as a goal assumes that the most important thing about employees is their health status, not their ability to do the job. I myself, in the days when I actually used to be entrusted to run companies with actual people in them other than myself, found no correlation between ability/productivity and health status, and would never have dreamed of creating a culture that would focus front-and-center on health. The culture I created was to have fun. So when we had company outings there were, of course, physical events, but there were also games, so that no one felt left out. If you've read this far into *Why Nobody Believes*, you won't be shocked to hear we also had trivia contests.

hypothetical, if your cafeteria made all their entrees out of tofu, your employees would be healthier but they would also be in a pretty sour mood after lunch.

So, what is described below should improve health status, but never lose sight of the overall goal of being in business.

As coincidence would have it, I am writing these paragraphs while on vacation in Boulder, Colorado, often ranked as the healthiest county in the United States. Boulder didn't get that way by helping smokers to quit or helping obese people to lose weight. (Ironically, the county itself actually uses a very conventional—and completely ineffective—vendored program for its own employees who fit those categories.)

No, Boulder got that way by creating a culture of health in which unhealthy people feel out of place, and either leave or don't move in. A second part of the equation is that it is easy to maintain one's health here, with myriad biking and hiking paths, as well as 50-meter public pools, a popular lake, a mountain biking park, and a culture of healthy eating that extends even to an organic pet food store.

The culture is so well accepted that the county's residents voted years ago to tax themselves in order to maintain and expand these recreational opportunities. The main bike path even has streetlights.

So, Boulder's experience suggests two things that completely contradict the conventional wisdom:

1. Wellness may impact recruiting/retention more than the ingrained bad health habits of current staff—and yet, the former is rarely measured.
2. If you create a culture of wellness, not only can you skip the costly incentives to get people to participate, but people will actually *pay* (in the broadest sense of the word) to participate. In Boulder's case, "pay" means "face higher housing prices than surrounding counties." In the case of corporations, it means perhaps "be willing to work longer hours," as we'll see below.

The third lesson of Boulder—that if you build a physical wellness infrastructure, people will use it—does not really contradict the conventional wisdom (few would argue against fitness facilities) but does suggest that resources dedicated to wellness may be better allocated to physical improvements than to incentives and telephonic coaching.

Now, let's turn to corporate America to see if the Boulder experience is replicated there. As it happens, there are many examples of companies that won't hire smokers. They've done the exact same math I've described above and concluded that it's simply much more cost-effective to address healthcare risk right in the recruitment process than through smoking cessation programs afterward. These companies, with their blunt-instrument approach, are no doubt reducing their health risk exposure, but this particular policy wouldn't really do anything to facilitate recruitment and retention. Very few people are more likely to apply for a job specifically because smokers aren't allowed to apply. And, of course, otherwise qualified smokers would have to find work elsewhere. That would mean, for example, that Barack Obama would not have been able to get a job in your organization. (We hear he's quit, but we don't believe it. Another reason self-reported HRAs are suspect.)

However, organizations that have "Boulderized" themselves to create a culture of wellness that makes healthy people *want* to work there—no incentives needed—are much fewer and farther between.

But before you say, "that's what we want to do," decide if you want to end up like Boulder. Fact is, some of your best employees may be so dedicated to their jobs, and so talented at them, that they don't care about patrolling their health and will be turned off by efforts to make them do so. An extreme example might be Bob Fosse in *All That Jazz*—perfectly willing to kill himself to create the best choreography Broadway had ever seen.

The goal is to be the most productive workplace, not the healthiest. Being the healthiest increases productivity, other things close to equal, but other things still have to be close to equal: You wouldn't fill a company with triathletes just to keep your health spending down, would you, if other people were better at their jobs?

Like the ongoing Ginger-versus-Maryann debate,* there is not a right or wrong position—the important thing is to have the discussion. Some organizations will want to espouse a Boulder model. Others won't. Most would say they want to be in the middle. Yet, sometimes being in the middle is harder than it sounds. You don't see too many moderates in Congress. And you don't see too many hermaphrodites anywhere. That's because a culture change needs a take-off point. You either totally commit to a new culture or people will figure out that you haven't committed to it. So if you want to be in the middle, take your soundings often to make sure you are succeeding.

You might say: "We can offer incentives for smoking cessation and weight loss, and that won't create a Boulder situation. We can stay in the middle."

You wish.

If the incentives are small they won't have much impact. If they are large, positive incentives, they may very well have an impact—attracting more people to your company who want to take advantage of them, and alienating people in your company who don't qualify for them because they are already thin non-smokers, possibly creating the need to then incentivize everyone else, too, to prevent the perception of unfairness. It's always easy to throw money at a problem but sometimes that easy solution creates more problems that require more money being thrown at them. Just look at the federal government, which subsidized home ownership for years. Now that housing prices have collapsed, it has to subsidize home ownership even more. Fuel is the same way. Years of subsidizing fossil fuels means the "clean energy" sector now needs to be subsidized too, just to keep up.

So in your attempt to be fair, you might very well end up subsidizing everyone, impacting your overall profit.

---

*Maryann. Not even a close question if you ask me. And yet, some of the most world's most learned scholars would beg to differ.

None of this is to say that you *shouldn't* try to create a culture of wellness, or incentivize healthy behavior, or whatever else you like. Rather, the message is that nothing is that simple or obvious, or people would already be doing it.

Now, let's turn to the case study. This case study is for a Bay Area company in the software field. It doesn't want its name used because of the possibility that they might be hit with some kind of lawsuit by disclosing this stuff. I've tried to explain to the HR guy that smokers are not a minority protected by the Americans with Disabilities Act, the Fourteenth Amendment, or even the Cone of Silence, but try explaining that to someone whose stock options are going to vest if he can hang around another six months. So my data comes from line employees, rather than official channels.

Some of you are no doubt more familiar with tech culture than others and may find what I am about to say to be an oversimplification, but basically, techie types fit into two categories:

1. Much healthier than you or I
2. Much unhealthier than you or I

Whatever else you say about them, people devoted to technology are rarely average in any respect. For many years this company had mid-range medical claims, which for a tech company is not a good thing. Companies in this industry, like this one, tend to be much younger and much more male than average, those variables together usually being predictive of low claims. Their claims were bumped back up to midrange by their culture. The company was literally divided by floors into smokers and non-smokers, and smokers felt very welcome.

Before switching to a more open design, glass walls separated workspaces, but there was so much smoking on the second floor that it's only a slight exaggeration to say you couldn't see through the glass. And one non-smoking employee told me that when he got home, his wife could always tell just by the smell whether or not he had ventured upstairs even for a few minutes that day. "Once I had a long meeting with a non-smoker who had come from a long meeting on the smoking floor, and even then she could smell the smoke," he recounted. "I made a mental note that if I ever had an affair, I'd better do it with a non-smoker."

This was a vestige of the days when you could smoke at work, but the culture and the separation by floors remained long after smokers were forced outdoors. No one thought twice about it, and certainly no one tried to get smokers to quit. And despite their much higher claims cost and absenteeism—as well as the productivity loss of having to step outside for 10 minutes every hour or two once the rules changed about workplace smoking—no one ever thought about firing them. Techies are an intense crowd and smoking comes with intensity. It was routine for some of them to work around the clock, stopping only for smoking breaks and candy bars. You would never get rid of them (meaning the smokers) just to reduce your healthcare spending.

Then, in 1997, something happened. It wasn't planned at all, and it certainly wasn't planned as a wellness strategy. In fact, the newly hired vice president of operations, the guy who unknowingly tripped the wellness wire, had never even heard of wellness, for the simple reason that 15 years ago, wellness programs as such practically didn't exist. The new guy was, however, a major Ultimate Frisbee player. (For those who have never heard of the sport, imagine Frisbee-tossing meets Iwo Jima.) And, as luck would have it, this company abutted a municipal sports field that, though used extensively on weekends, was rarely used during the day during the week.

He started organizing Ultimate games during lunchtime. The first floor crowd, some of whom had played before, turned out in droves. Soon, two fields were needed. Then, they started playing after work, with "after work" defined as "between 5 p.m. and sunset," at which point many of them headed back to do more of whatever it is that techie people do.

What happened next (with "next" defined as "over a period of about 10 years") was that the Frisbee players started recruiting their friends to work there. This wasn't hard—some huge percentage of Ultimate Frisbee players are techies. Recruiting expense fell in this competitive market as people found the company rather than the reverse. The company top brass, finally realizing that they were onto something (another reason that they didn't want their name used is that the people who ran the place weren't exactly visionary, according to my sources) paid the town to leave the lights on later into the evening, and also paid for the installation of artificial turf, albeit somewhat under duress, after it became clear who was chewing up the field.

You're probably wondering what the heck all of this actually did to healthcare expenses given that this is a book about health expenses. Their healthcare spending is now about 30 percent lower than average—a dramatic improvement over the 15-year period.

It's not hard to see why if you visit the place. The smokers' ranks have been greatly diminished, not because they quit smoking or someone fired them, but because they got marginalized by the new culture. Almost every smoker who left was replaced by a Frisbee player, virtually none of whom smoke. My friend—the guy who fed me this information (in addition to what I was able to glean myself, having joined them in a few pickup games)—says he never smells like smoke any more. And, no, he isn't having an affair with a non-smoker, either. ("I figure if the wife could smell smoke she could smell perfume.")

A Wellness Program That People Are Willing to Pay For?

As this chapter shows, people "pay" to be in a culture of wellness. Yet, of the 150 wellness companies in the universe, 149 of them require being subsidized or otherwise incentivized by the boss in order to work. Despite this chapter's lessons, there is only one (in addition to bricks-and-mortar programs and weight-loss classes like Jenny Craig) that starts with a track record of consumers *paying them for the privilege* of taking their program. That's a company called www.StickK.com. StickK allows you to make "commitment contracts," in which you bet against yourself to complete an unpleasant task. One example—this one made *All Things Considered*—is worth

1,000 words of my increasingly grating prose. A civil rights leader committed to give the Ku Klux Klan $5,000 if she couldn't stop smoking. And she did. Close to 150,000 people have paid StickK—not much, but paid them nonetheless—to set up, monitor, and referee those contracts online.

Why? Because they see the value and are willing to pay for it. That should be the talisman of wellness for any program: You may still want to subsidize employees, but the program should have enough value on its own merits to be attractive to consumers even before any subsidies are applied.

Commentator Linda Riddell, writing one of the most thoughtful wellness commentaries I've ever read (it's on the *Employee Benefit News* blog), sums it up far more gracefully than I: Besides being cheaper, programs that channel "intrinsic motivation" into actions will far outperform those relying on "financial motivation" for results. StickK clearly falls in the first category.

Chapter 6

Yes, Virginia, There Is a Savings Clause

I t's tough to read much of *Why Nobody Believes* without reaching for the Prozac or perhaps the generic equivalent thereof. The good news is that, recalling the engineering adage about the bridges, we have found a few that do stay up. For instance, Chapter 2 included an example of an asthma program, sponsored by Harvard Pilgrim, that reduced asthma admissions and ER visits even as the leading newspaper in the same region was bemoaning the regional increase in asthma. Chapter 5 described two wellness solutions that work, though the second would be difficult to replicate while the first necessarily requires patience in cost-savings expectations, along the lines of the Highmark model.

By the way, the second program isn't alone in requiring patience: All successful wellness programs aimed at health improvement require patience. Most simply try to hide that fact with wishful thinking multipliers showing massive, albeit non-existent, savings in the near/intermediate term.

We have found only one vendor that does save money in the near/intermediate term, and this chapter will dissect it. Patience is therefore less of an issue with this vendor than in wellness, but this vendor's program requires willingness to actively manage both the health benefit and the carrier. The reward for doing those two things: a program that works.

This chapter will describe not just *that* the program works—plenty of companies say they instituted a population health improvement (PHI) program and their costs fell the next year—but additionally, how you know the result in this case isn't attributable to just good fortune or good demographics. What you are about to read about is also guaranteeable: The vendor that helped to produce these outcomes will offer a "Savings Clause," a contractual clause guaranteeing savings.

The organization in this case study is the City of Savannah, Georgia. Savannah has an aging workforce with a very high rate of diabetes and related complications, a problem typical to the southeastern region of the United States in general and municipal workforces in particular.

A diabetic disease management program had previously been implemented where members willing to participate in a hospital-based diabetes education program could enjoy a low, global co-pay for all of their diabetes-related treatments as well as routine exams.

Savannah also had a wellness screening program for employees, a program whose participation levels and outcomes were consistently disappointing. The city continued to experience annual increases in medical spending exceeding benchmarks. Enter Quantum Health.

Here is a snapshot of Quantum Health (QH). Because the Quantum model is a bit square-peg-in-round-holish, the "snapshot" by necessity chews up five paragraphs, so bear with me.

For starters, the Quantum model would fall into the PHI category of care coordination. (See the Glossary.) While care coordination involves multiple goals, the three most important would be:

1. Keeping people inside the system to control utilization of specialists, and the high-priced diagnostics and procedures that often accompany or follow specialist visits.
2. Avoiding duplication of those diagnostics.
3. Identifying candidates for disease management when people are *ready to change* to avoid acute events rather than respond to them.

All of those goals get accomplished in large part because QH tweaks the benefits design to encourage inbound calling at appropriate times—and provides the member services component of health benefit administration as well as the population health improvement components, meaning that all these calls come to QH and get triaged by QH. The benefit design tweaks mean QH receives about three times the call volume that a typical health plan would get. Nothing onerous is involved here: Members who need a specialist, for example, qualify for a lower co-pay if they or their primary physician call in for a referral, rather than just making an appointment on their own.

Note: These changes—really just tweaks—to the benefits design don't increase employee share of expense. The tweaks simply move the numbers around so that employees who play by the rules spend less money than they would have. It's a real-life example of the old joke that salespeople tell, about the three biggest lies, the punchline of which is: "You can actually make more money under the new system." Other tweaks include incentives to see a primary care physician and engage in preventive screening.

When a covered employee's call comes in, QH doesn't treat it like a typical health plan would, where the idea is to answer the phone quickly, answer the question quickly (and politely, of course), and move onto the next call. Whereas a typical health plan treats inbound calls as an inconvenience, QH treats them as an opportunity. Assisted by prompted software support questions, the member services people determine whether and who to triage to wellness, disease management, case management, or other functions. So, for instance, a member calling in for a referral to a cardiologist might be asked if he would like to talk to someone about heart health.

Perhaps the best real-life example is one that took place when I myself was on a site tour. A new employee of a QH customer called to ask if diabetic shoes were a covered benefit. Whereas most health plan member services representatives would have answered the question and moved on, this caller was transferred directly into a diabetes disease management program. Had this caller been in an ordinary health plan, he would not have been identified for a disease management program until after (usually well after) he incurred a claim—and that claim would likely be an expensive one, given that his diabetes was already advanced enough that he was requesting information about shoes. By contrast, QH enrolled the caller in disease management even before he incurred his first findable claim. This was not a coincidence, due to the tweaks mentioned above that generate such a high volume of incoming calls.

Back to the City of Savannah. Like most self-funded employers with some kind of population management program, they compare themselves to the what-would-have-been trend—without, of course, knowing the what-would-have-been trend. Nine times out of 10—as in the Georgia and North Carolina Medicaid examples—massive savings can be reported versus trend even though it might later turn out that the program hadn't actually done anything.

Based on that comparison to trend, the Savannah results look like anyone else's. Since most consultants and vendors don't plausibility-check savings versus trend, had Savannah stopped with the announcement of savings-vs.-trend, there would be nothing remarkable about the result. I probably would have ranted about how it was a perfect example of how people never plausibility-check their numbers.

However, in this case, the plausibility was carefully checked. Utilization of various types of resources was checked to make sure that the alleged decline in spending versus trend was not due to overestimating trend, but rather to actual reduction of utilization. Recall the *every metric can't improve* rule: If the cost of *everything* appears to go down, the inflation trend adjustment must be wrong, because—our mantra—while insulating your house saves money, the cost of insulation goes up.

Clearly, Beth Robinson, human resources director for Savannah, has enjoyed the results. "Since implementing the Quantum model in 2007, our claims trend is essentially flat . . . and that's a drop of more than 10 points from where it was in the past. We're proud that we have saved the taxpayers of the City of Savannah millions of dollars over that time through effective case management, high touch care coordination, and successfully engaging more employees in managing their health."

There is a corollary to the cost-of-everything-going-down observation even if there is no inflation trending, meaning even if the metrics are purely utilization-based. The corollary is that, just as with cost, if *utilization* of everything goes down, then the population changed or the co-pays changed or something happened not related to the PHI program. The utilization expectation of a care coordination program specifically involving the benefits design changes necessary to support such a program would be as follows:

Category of Resource Use	Expected Direction of Utilization
Primary care visits	Up
Use of outpatient services other than primary care (specialist, OP diagnostics, OP surgeries)	Down
Inpatient utilization	Down
Disease management program participation	Up

Now, let's compare to actual changes for Savannah, to plausibility-test the expected changes:

Category of Resource Use	Expected Direction	Actual Change
Primary care visits	Up	+13%
Other outpatient services	Down	−5%
Inpatient utilization	Down	−6%
Disease management program participation	Up	+300%

The result: Directional and magnitudinal changes are in line with expectations for each of the four categories of resource use. Even so, one should check all other explanations, as well. The sidebar, which can be applied to your own situation, contains eight other possible explanations for improved trend or utilization, which need to be totally or largely ruled out as causes of that improved trend before crediting the improvement to any program. The Savannah results were not infected by any of the potential alternative explanations in the sidebar.

Rounding Up the Usual Suspects—and Then Letting Them Go

When there is a significant change in spending versus trend— on the off-chance that the trend was correctly calculated—the change can be attributed to one or more of the following factors. All were reviewed and easily ruled out as contributing to Savannah's performance.

Plan Design/Access Impediments

Client did not cost shift to employees—in fact, plan design netted a 0.5 percent enhancement in benefits. Benefits were enhanced to reinforce office visits to the PCP and provided an incentive for PCP usage as well as PCP notification to Quantum Health for specialty referral.

Contribution Methodology

Employee contribution to health spending did not change, though independent adjustments were made per a few union contracts. Contributions and plan eligibility were not tied to participation. Because of cost savings, actual out-of-pocket cost to the employees went down.

Demographics

There was a 23 percent increase in portion of members more than 40 years of age, which is consistent with the average increase in the DMPC database.

Labor Force Change

City employee staff grew by about 20 percent from Year 0 to Year 3. There were no layoffs or consolidations during this period. There was no "merger" with other municipalities, no early retiree payouts, and no change in statutory hiring preferences.

Network Discounts/Vendors

No change.

Management Involvement

There was no step-function change in management involvement and no change in vocal or visible support for improved health management beyond the publication of plan design changes.

Large Cost Increase in Previous Year

Especially in smaller organizations, healthcare cost increases don't follow a straight line. A large increase may be followed by a small increase, and it is often tempting to assume that the large increase is a trend, not a blip, and that any improvement must be attributable to an intervention. In this case, costs had been rising steadily.

Multi-Site Operations Where Some Sites' Cost Increased More Than Other Sites

Savannah applied QH across the board so this doesn't apply. The general rule is: If some of your sites' healthcare costs increased more than others did last year, don't apply an intervention only to those sites and then compare subsequent performance to the sites whose costs had not been increasing. However, if some sites are chronically higher-cost than others, an intervention applied to those sites would show valid results.

Of course, nothing this effective is going to be easy—those two categories of adjective are mutually exclusive in PHI. There are two specific asterisks that move this intervention from the "easy" category into the "effective" category. First, unlike other, generally ineffective, PHI interventions, you actually have to *do something* other than spend money to make this work. You need to be willing to tweak your benefits design to align it with the QH philosophy of encouraging people to call in. This can involve an increase in employer share, if employee relations are such that you can't just increase co-pays in some areas while reducing them in others. You may need to settle for reducing employee co-pays for pre-approved referrals and testing, which starts you out in the hole. (This was the case in Savannah but the city saved money nonetheless.)

Second, you need to take back the member services function from the carrier. If you are following the straightforward and obvious how-to contractual guidelines in Chapter 8, you're all set up for this. Naturally you aren't, but unless you are negotiating a carrier contract right this very moment, in which case you should skip Chapter 7 and jump to Chapter 8, we'd recommend reading all the chapters. If for no other reason than you paid for all the chapters.

Chapter 7

Disease Management Programs That Actually Work (Pinch Me)

Quantum, though clearly an effective program (and one that I personally have written auditors' letters for, guaranteeing their validity), requires breaking eggs to make omelets. Their program can't just be overlaid onto an existing health benefit. The best wellness programs, described in Chapter 5, do "move the needle" more than just HRAs and some coaching would do, but it takes years to translate movements of the needle into cost savings, as the Highmark example shows. So that brings us back to disease management, as the only genre of program that can find savings in the nearish term noiselessly. Even then, note that none of what follows are outbound call-center-only models, just like none of the notable wellness programs are simple HRA-plus-coaching models, both of which require limited effort to implement. Instead, one example below is a combination DM/wellness/benefit design program. Two are programs in which the health plan and the doctors are joined at the hip. The last requires a serious investment.

Combined DM/Wellness/Incentives/Benefits Redesign: How Doing All Four in Coordination Creates Synergy

Earlier in *Why Nobody Believes* we talked about the folly of trying to measure the impact of one program, like disease management or wellness, when you are doing both, especially when you are also changing benefits design.

Even if parsing out the impact is harder, some companies have learned that undertaking all these initiatives together, in a coordinated way, will have much more impact than doing them individually, sort of like Reese's Cups. While peanut butter was invented in 1890 and the chocolate bar was invented in 1920, Reese's Cups weren't invented until 1963. Yes, it took 43 years before someone eating a chocolate bar fell into a manhole right on top of someone who was eating peanut butter. Remarkably, no one was injured, and as luck would have it, a professional camera crew was on hand to record the scene.

In this case, a consumer products company with 32,000 U.S. employees, whose population health programs have subsequently won awards, synergized its benefits and disease management/wellness strategies to achieve the Reese's Cup of employee health and spending—a much better outcome than changing either of the components alone would have created. Their longtime partner who gets credited for a major assist on this performance is Alere, a very fine vendor whose integrity is confirmed by the fact that, aside from this vignette, they have managed to keep their name out of this book, a stunning achievement shared by few of their peers.

The company itself can't be disclosed even though the HR department would like to reveal this information. Unfortunately, this organization's internal process for allowing name disclosure is complex enough to make the process for getting FDA approval for a biotech drug look like renewing a car registration online. The company's HR department wasn't even allowed to review this chapter ahead of time, so that if I get any of the story wrong, they not only get to keep their hands clean but also, if necessary, deny my very existence.

Like Moe and Larry when the sergeant asked for a volunteer to step forward for a suicide mission, let's take a step back. In our case, that means looking at the program's conception and evolution over time. The first order of business, in 2005, was a comprehensive health assessment of the employee population. Not surprisingly, for an "old economy" company, the finding was that as compared with the U.S. population as a whole, the employees had a higher percentage of just about everything one would prefer not to have a higher percentage of. Equally unsurprisingly, the company's adverse event rates were also higher than average. Together, these findings created a call to action.

At this point, most HR types would just have "put in a program" and called it a day, relying on their benefits consultants both to show them how much money they could claim to have saved and to provide them with slides and figures that they could use to perpetuate these mythical savings to their senior management. This company opted to take a different path, starting with financing these initiatives not by claiming nonexistent savings but rather by reconfiguring their benefits design so that the employees' and company's interests would be better aligned while savings were being generated. Specifically, they significantly increased co-pays for Viagra-like drugs that they considered to be the most employee-centric and the least likely to enhance productivity:

- Acne treatments
- Hormonal replacements
- Contraceptives
- Non-sedating antihistamines
- Adult ADD treatments
- Antifungals
- Infertility treatments
- Sedative hypnotics

By doing so, they were able to finance wellness and disease management, and reduce or eliminate the co-pays for drugs and other subsidies supporting those programs. It doesn't do any good for a disease manager to tell a financially strapped employee to comply with drugs if the drug co-pays over the course of a year might reach $600, as is the case in asthma, where most of the drugs are name-brand and hence expensive using the typical tiered drug co-pay system. Conversely, it doesn't do any good to reduce co-pays for asthma controller medications to almost nothing and expect people to automatically start filling scripts. Doing both together, however, is a Reese's Cup.

After finalizing adjustments to the medical and prescription benefits in 2006, the company developed an integrated, comprehensive set of health and wellness programs with strong financial incentives and a communications plan to generate high participation rates. They also wanted a program that would help employees become wise healthcare consumers. "To have the healthiest people, we knew we needed to engage them," said a senior benefits leader.

The company selected Alere because it wanted to avoid working with multiple vendors. Alere could offer all of the programs the company needed on one platform. Not just chronic care programs (for asthma, chronic obstructive pulmonary disease, diabetes, coronary artery disease, heart failure, musculoskeletal and pain problems, and depression) but also a wellness suite. The latter included a health portal, health/productivity assessment, and online, six-week healthy living programs, which employees could complete in their own time.

Wellness and DM are most likely to pay for themselves in situations like this one: aging workforces with low turnover. "We knew that it would be less expensive for us to keep people healthy rather than wait for them to become ill and then have to pay for their illness," the senior benefits leader said. "And we owe them this for their years of service anyway."

To promote engagement, the company used the pot of money they collected on lifestyle drug co-pays to finance a generous incentive plan that included $100 for wellness assessment completion, $100 for completion of a healthy living program, $200 for enrollment in a disease management program, and another $200 on the anniversary date of enrollment. Employees who participated in the company-wide wellness challenge would be entered into a year-end drawing to exempt 175 winners from paying the following year's health insurance premium.

Even with all those incentives, the company did not take a laissez-faire, if-you-bribe-them-they-will-come approach to communications. "We knew we had to win their hearts as well as wallets, and we couldn't inspire them if we presented the programs as a cost saving measure for the company," said the senior benefits leader. "We knew our approach should be that 'we are here to help you get healthier—we want to be focused on you being as healthy as possible.'"

The combination of these four programs (co-pays, wellness, disease management, and incentives, for those of you keeping score at home) has generated a steady reduction in chronic disease events, measured validly on Figure 7.1. That's the good news. The bad news—which really isn't so bad in the overall scheme of things (sort of like having to pay a lot of income tax on April 15 because you made more money than you expected to make the previous year)—is that it's impossible to distinguish the impact of one of these four programs from the other three. The combination has reduced events quite a bit, but which leg of the stool bore the most weight will forever be a mystery.

The astute observer might notice in Figure 7.1 that heart failure and COPD events have hardly budged. That could be considered a disappointment, except that the percentage of employees at this company over age 50 rose by 45 percent over that period and currently represents about 30 percent of total employee population. In that context, these programs' ability to hold back the heart failure and COPD tides was worthy of King Canute himself.

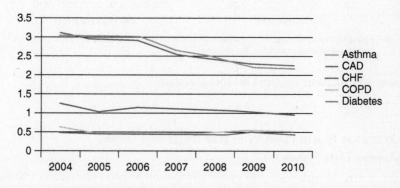

FIGURE 7.1   Event Rate Trends at Consumer Goods Company per 1,000 Covered Lives

It's much easier to tell if a program didn't work than if it did, because the intermediate quality indicators would show no change. Quite the contrary in this case:

- ◆ 82 percent of disease-eligible employees enrolled in disease management programs (in contrast to the usual 15 to 20 percent).
- ◆ Medication compliance rose across the board. Figure 7.2 illustrates the steady and substantial reduction in non-compliance since program inception.

By now, six years into the program, wellness can be measured much more on companywide risk factor improvement than participation rates. Total risk factors have fallen by 13 percent even as the company has aged rapidly. Specific improvements contributing to the net risk reduction are listed on Figure 7.3 on page 159.

Non-compliant Members as a Percent of Total Diabetic Utilizers

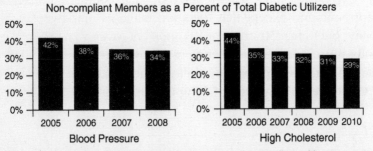

Blood Pressure   High Cholesterol

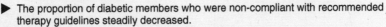

▶ The proportion of diabetic members who were non-compliant with recommended therapy guidelines steadily decreased.

FIGURE 7.2 Diabetic Gaps in Care for Cholesterol

SUCCESSES AT HEALTH PLANS WHO PLAY NICELY WITH OTHERS (MEANING THEIR PROVIDERS)

Americans' health status is generally better in blue states than in red ones.

That better health status, specifically in Oregon and Massachusetts, *is already taken into account* in the following vignettes

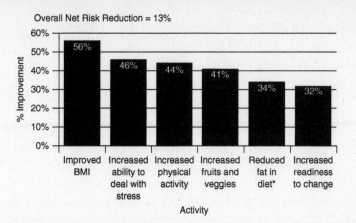

Overall Net Risk Reduction = 13%

FIGURE 7.3 Contributors to Risk Reduction

of successful health plan disease management programs, which are measured against their respective regions. So, when you read about their successes or the successes of other health plans in coastal states, don't think: "Well, of course their program was successful because they are headquartered in [insert name of state so blue that they even voted for that dweeb in the tank]."

How can you tell? First, the rate of improvement over the decade *relative to everyone else* was quite impressive, even though the demographics of these states haven't changed relative to everyone else over that period. For instance, given half a chance most of these states would *still* vote for that dweeb in the tank. Second, we put in a line to reflect the regional averages for New England and the Pacific Northwest. This is based on our databases but can easily be roughly confirmed through that mother of all databases, HCUP.

If not due to geography, what is the most likely reason for their success? Note in the sidebar that regional plans—especially those that are provider-owned and/or provider-centric—dominate the list of plans achieving good enough outcomes to be recognized as "best health plans" in the *10th Annual Report on the Disease Management and Wellness Industries* (2012).

---

*It would appear, ironically, that fewer Reese's Cups are being consumed.

Highlights from the *10th Annual Report on the Disease Management and Wellness Industries*

Because it would be immature of us and hurtful to them, we would never, ever, in a million years ever dream of disclosing the names of the anonymized organizations used as case studies in *Why Nobody Believes* (well, at least not for free). However, we are happy to disclose the names of the organizations that have won awards for validity and event rate reduction in 2012's *10th Annual Report on the Disease Management and Wellness Industries*, either by applying or by presenting valid outcomes at a conference. If yours is on this list, great. If not, you either flunked or you didn't apply. If the latter, you might as well apply. It's not like it costs anything and it's quite easy. All you need to do is submit at least five years' event rates on the official template and see if your rates outperformed the averages.

This list is periodically updated on www.dismgmt.com.

Health Plans
> Amerihealth Mercy
> Blue Care Network of Michigan
> Blue Cross of Alabama
> Blue Cross of Delaware
> Blue Cross of Massachusetts
> Blue Cross of Northeastern Pennsylvania
> Blue Cross of Rhode Island
> Blue Cross of Vermont
> Boston Medical Center Health Plan
> Capital District Physicians Health Plan
> CareFirst BlueCross BlueShield
> ConnectiCare
> Fallon Community Health Plan
> Harvard Pilgrim Health Care

Health Alliance Medical Plan
Health Alliance Plan
HealthPartners
LACare
PreferredOne
Providence Health Plan
Scott & White Health Plan
Summacare
WPS Health Insurance

States

Ohio (OPERS and STRS only)
Utah (Public Employees Health Plan)
Wyoming Medicaid

Employers

Boston College
Cisco
City of Savannah
John Hancock
Oshkosh Corporation
Procter & Gamble
Terex
Worthington Industries

This list might explain why focused local plans stay in business despite a lack of scale economies: It's that they really do provide a better outcome for their population because doctors are less likely to think of them as an insurer and more likely to think of them as a partner. The two plans highlighted here show how most of the plans on this list utilize this partnership.

HARVARD PILGRIM HEALTH CARE

Harvard Pilgrim Health Care (HPHC), already mentioned earlier in the context of its asthma program, has enjoyed success in other conditions as well as that one. However, I'm going to expand on HPHC because, to paraphrase the immortal words of the great philosopher Sy Sperling, I'm not just a writer about HPHC. I'm also a client. And my son had asthma. (Still does, but those of you who are parents out there, take heart. I'm not sure it ever "goes away," but what they say is true: As your kids grow and their airways expand, inflammation is much less debilitating, if even noticeable.)

When he first got it, we didn't guess that he had it—no family history, no overstuffed furniture or shag carpeting, and no cats. We treated his condition at first by the tried-and-true method of saying: "Paul, stop coughing."

Eventually, he landed in the ER, where it was diagnosed (a classic "tails" moving to "heads"). We took him to the pediatrician for a follow-up visit. The pediatrician said: "The bad news is, he has asthma. The good news is, I just went to a Harvard Pilgrim session, where they showed us how children can now be medicated very conveniently using inhalers instead of nebulizers for 20 minutes, with equal or better effectiveness." Can you imagine that conversation happening with most health plans?

This was not an isolated event. HPHC has always had its providers' attention both because of panel size and because it has roots in the community, having been founded by physicians and, for many years, run by physicians recruited from its own network.

On the member side, Harvard Pilgrim is also quite conscientious. Just as advertised, they did indeed call us after my son's ER visit and answered our questions about managing his asthma. The materials we received in the mail focused on pediatric asthma, not asthma generally, and were up to date enough to be synced with the new inhaler protocols the pediatrician had mentioned.

HPHC has other clear points of differentiation, as well. They focus on people who appear out of control of their health generally, and only secondarily look at the condition, whereas the CCA guidelines and most vendors start with specific algorithms designed to ferret out people with the condition. That approach misses people who are baffled by their inability to get a diagnosis or control their disease. Harvard Pilgrim finds those folks, identifiable by their use of multiple specialists and attendant multiple diagnostics and prescriptions—and only then looks to see what disease(s) they might have. This is precisely the opposite of traditional disease management. The 131-page CCA guidelines, for example, don't even mention the word "specialist," while "prescriptions" appears only once in an unrelated context.

When they talk to members, HPHC does two things that most others don't. First, they don't use prepared scripts, which sound, well, like prepared scripts. Nurses using scripts always seem to be trying to make points, rather than actually engaging the member. Think of Al Gore versus George W. Bush in the 2000 presidential debates. Gore made all the points, but Bush sounded like the guy you'd rather hang out with, meaning he won the debate because we all want a president we can hang out with. (Like that worked.)

Instead of checking off points on a scripted agenda, HPHC's nurses focus on what's important to the member. As Catherine McFayden, director of their disease management program, said: "We guide and noodge, but we don't set the agenda. Otherwise, you don't get behavior change. That's why we don't use scripts."

On the other hand, they do use guidelines to make sure the points get covered. That avoids nurses straying too far in the other direction, like another vendor that is well known for emphasizing relationship building rather than scripted calls. A conversation conducted by one of the latter's nurses was described to me by a client listening in on a call: "At the end of 15 minutes, we still didn't know the member's HbA1c, but we knew the name of her dog."

Finally, HPHC, in sharp contrast to almost everybody, has the actual nurses making the outbound calls. "You can lose a lot of people in a call transfer, and it sounds much more supportive to be called by the person whom you are actually going to talk to."

Event rates over time—the only true measure of outcomes—are seen in Figure 7.4.

PROVIDENCE HEALTH PLAN

Harvard Pilgrim is just one example of a pattern: As can be seen from the previous sidebar, with the exception of some Blues, provider-owned health plans dominate the list of leading health plans in disease management like steroid users dominate the list of baseball's leading home-run hitters. The difference is that the former use more drugs.

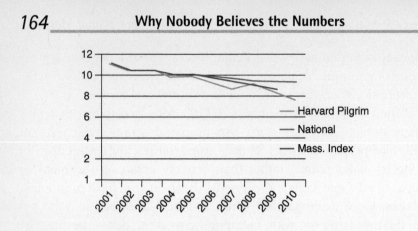

FIGURE 7.4 Event Rates per 1,000 People

Note: The "Mass. Index" is based on public data from the HCUP database, which, though excellent in other respects, is not exactly updated in Internet time. Therefore, as mentioned earlier, 2010 data was not available before we went to press in 2012.

For example, Providence Health Plan ranks as perhaps the country's leader in overall drug adherence in the Medicare population. A look at its CHF adherence ratios shows adherence rates pushing up against that magic 100 percent mark; the level beyond it is impossible to go. See Figure 7.5. (Presumably by now most of you believe me when I say that.)

They also get tested more often than baseball players do (see Figure 7.6).

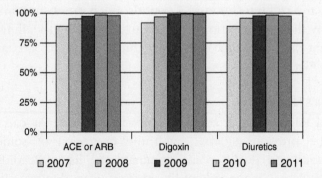

FIGURE 7.5 HEDIS—Medicare Congestive Heart Failure Measures: Annual Monitoring for Patients on Persistent Medications

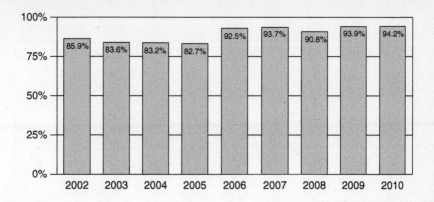

FIGURE 7.6 Lipid Screening for Cardiovascular Conditions: Medicare HEDIS Scores

As a result, Providence has achieved four stars for Medicare Part C and five stars for Part D. (One place where there is no grade inflation is Medicare, which as of this writing has awarded four or five stars to less than 5 percent of all Medicare Advantage plans.) The conscientiousness of health plan management has paid off both in retention rates, and more importantly, in days per 1,000 as shown in Figure 7.7.

The improvement has come disproportionately from chronic disease events, which have consistently declined in the PHP Medicare population as shown in Figure 7.8.

How do they do it? Well, if you just read the Quantum Health and Harvard Pilgrim case studies, some of what follows will sound like, to quote the immortal words of the great philosopher Yogi Berra, "déjà vu all over again." In other words, certain themes run through successful programs.

People known to be sick are fast-tracked into programs. In the case of Providence, patients admitted to hospitals are connected with care managers* almost immediately upon discharge, when they are

---

*In this case, *care manager* is a catchall term for case manager, disease manager, or complex case manager. Believe it or not, those are all different terms. That's why I included a Glossary with *Why Nobody Believes* (plus I thought that would make it easier to sell the movie rights).

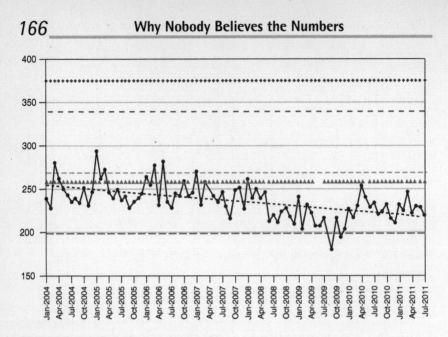

Figure 7.7 Annualized Hospital Admits per 1,000 Medicare Members versus Benchmarks

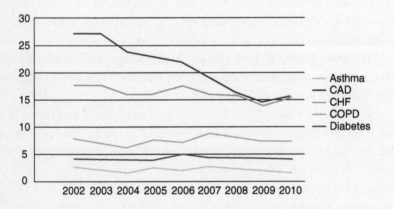

Figure 7.8 Chronic Disease Rates per 1,000 Medicare Members

likely most receptive to ideas for health improvement—no need to wait months for claims to show up and be processed before contact is made.

And just as disease managers at Quantum Health are co-located with member services, at Providence these various types of care

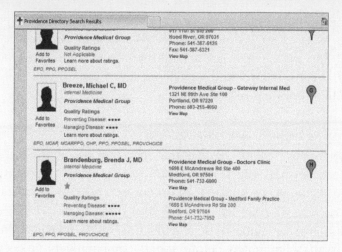

FIGURE 7.9   Sample of Providence Online Physician Ratings

manager are co-located with one another, so that people can easily be transitioned as their circumstances change. Like Harvard Pilgrim, the nurses make all the calls personally—no intermediaries and none of those annoying silences after picking up the phone that people now know to associate with telemarketing.

While some health plans publish the satisfaction statistics for doctors, Providence may be unique in putting statistics for "preventing disease" and "managing disease" right online. Yes, you read that right. Don't take my word for it – here, as shown in Figure 7.9, is a sample pulled right off the web. You can imagine the motivational impact on the doctors.

One advantage of doing your own disease management for mostly your own members and only a few other large accounts is that it is easy to evolve the program. You aren't locked into a whole bunch of overwrought, uber-detailed, and consultant-generated contracts, as described earlier.

Providence has used this flexibility fully and constantly evaluates and improves its assessment tool, reducing the number of questions while increasing the actionability of that first interaction, so that people want to be re-contacted. For instance, handling people's questions about drug adherence or generic substitution, or teaching them how to "know your numbers" is much more likely to leave a good impression than just asking them a gazillion questions that they've already been asked a gazillion times just so you can satisfy contractual reporting requirements.

A SUCCESS REQUIRING SIGNIFICANT INVESTMENT

Ever noticed at a shopping mall that there are few mid-sized stores? There are several "big box" anchor stores, and a whole slew of boutique-type places staffed with one or two people—but not much in between, giving the latter a high ROI due to the low investment required. It's the same with population health management. The health plans highlighted before spend comparatively little on DM, but spend it wisely. The next example requires a serious commitment to DM, quite a bit more than a typical program costs. And yet that works, too. Perhaps it's the typical mid-range programs that may be mis-sized.

The most intensive population health management program ever?

Benjamin Disraeli observed that there were two things that people should never see being made—sausages and laws. If he were around today, he could have added a third: Medicare disease management demonstration projects. The one undertaken in 2005 to 2006 found that only two of eight sites showed significant reductions in hospital admissions, and none showed significant reductions in costs. Newspaper headlines the next day were unequivocal—summed up by one declaring, "Medicare Disease Management Pilot Failed."[1]

In the ensuing weeks, industry buzz revealed a back-story that set an intriguing context for the CMS project. According to some, the powerful government agency—skeptical of disease management strategies—had saddled the project with its sickest patients who, in the words of one study participant, were "past the point where any supports or interventions would make a difference." On top of that, patient data provided by CMS—the lifeblood of effective disease management—was often incomplete or reported too late to be actionable.

Nevertheless, a public verdict had been rendered. But two industry pioneers weren't about to let it go unanswered: George Bennett, PhD, co-founder of Health Dialog and a relentless proponent of the power of deep data and quality interventions to impact costs; and David Wennberg, MD, MPH, who with his father, John Wennberg, MD, MPH, and a team at Dartmouth changed the face of health care by establishing how health care providers behave very differently depending on where they are geographically located, causing patients to get care—often costly—that they may not need or want.

Bennett and Wennberg, in collaboration with their colleagues at Health Dialog, resolved to do their own cost study—one that was larger, with better methodology, using the best interventions, and directed to people who could be helped.

Two health plans—both Health Dialog clients—were enlisted to cooperate. With 174,120 eligible subjects (following exclusions for obvious reasons, like dropping the plan or already having rare high-cost conditions like ESRD), this would be the largest study of its kind. The study was designed so that baseline medical costs and resource utilization would be similar for both groups. Using a stratified random sample design, a combination of conditions and risks created several similar groups, and then individuals within these groups were randomized into the usual and enhanced groups.

To say that I am not exactly a huge predictive modeling fan is like saying that Benjamin Netenyahu is not a huge Hamas fan. Predictive modeling simply oozes regression to the mean, in that the models basically just dress up last year's high-cost members with a financial "risk score" based on last year's high cost—and guess what? Their cost and risk scores decline in subsequent years. However, this study used predictive modeling not to "predict cost" and then show fictitious savings against the prediction, but rather it used predictive models to identify members who could most benefit from health coaching, with a focus on finding enhanced group members *already assigned to the study group* most likely to experience expensive episodes of care. The outcomes, however, were assessed on the total randomized groups.

Hey, Butch, Who Are Those Guys?

Health Dialog's approach to care management centers on providing people with unbiased information to help them manage their health and care, including how to change behaviors and lifestyles, and choose treatment options that are right for them.

Health Dialog support is provided by trained health coaches—registered nurses, licensed vocational nurses, respiratory therapists, dietitians, and pharmacists—who teach self-care, motivate behavior change and treatment adherence, and enable people to work with their physicians to make treatment decisions based on their own values and need. Support tools are provided in coordination with health coaching in the form of web links, videos and DVDs, and publications.

Sophisticated and proprietary predictive modeling allows Health Dialog to actively reach those people within a plan's membership who can benefit from support, and reach them at a "teachable moment"—such as when a patient has just been discharged from the hospital, or when a person is facing a treatment decision.

According to the study design, the first group would receive the usual level of Health Dialog support and the number of individuals receiving support would be consistent with Health Dialog's historic practices (the "usual support group"); the individuals in the second group would receive more intensive support than those in the usual support group, and a greater percent of the individuals in the second group would receive support (the "enhanced support group"). The hypothesis was that the enhanced support group would show a higher reduction in cost trend.

RESULTS

The study measured cost of care by looking at subjects' use of hospital, emergency room, and outpatient services; and admissions for selected surgeries (prostate, hip, knee, back, uterine, coronary revascularization). Outcome measures were derived from insurance claims provided by the two participating health plans over a 12-month period.

Results from the study were published in *The New England Journal of Medicine (NEJM)*, a testament to the rigorous nature of the work. And recall that *NEJM* is not exactly a patsy for disease management outcomes—they were the ones who published the study showing that an intervention based on the Vendor A model saved nothing.

As compared to the usual support group, the enhanced support group showed a cost reduction of $7.96 per member per month, comprised of $8.48 in cost reductions minus* $0.52 pharmacy cost increase, the cost of improved medication adherence. This translates to 3.6 percent lower costs in the intervention group (enhanced support group) as compared to the usual support group.

All seven plausibility tests were passed. Most importantly and most subtly, the *nexus* and *quality dose–cost response* rules were satisfied. The utilization reductions showed up in the targeted categories, and almost all the HEDIS indicators improved, the majority by more than the cost reduction percentage.

THE SECRET SAUCE

Well, first of all, it's not called "secret sauce." How could sauce be a secret? It's staring at you right from the plate. Those old Big Mac ads were for *special* sauce, not secret sauce. For decades, people have been confusing McDonalds' special sauce with the even older KFC ad touting the "secret blend of 11 herbs and spices," and I for one am not going to stand for it any longer!

The special sauce (and if it was a secret, it isn't anymore) would be composed of the following:

1. *Consumer empowerment*. This intervention empowered individuals with a wide range of conditions, including but not

---

*You read that verb right: It's *minus* pharmacy cost. Seven chapters into *Why Nobody Believes*, someone is finally admitting that they need to insulate their house in order to save energy, the only problem being that "minus" isn't a verb. I'm not quite sure what it is, to be honest.

limited to chronic conditions, to participate in medical treatment decisions with their doctors. This contrasts with other programs, which focus narrowly on one or two disease-specific metrics such as closing a particular care gap.

2. *Shared decision-making.* Members received decision support through multimedia decision aids and coaching for key surgical decisions, which can drive costs, such as hip, knee, and back surgeries.

3. *Engagement.* The intervention engaged three times as many people (10.4 percent versus 3.7 percent) in the enhanced support group as compared to the usual support group, a much higher proportion of the population than most other programs.

4. *Unwarranted variation analytics.* Health Dialog has developed innovative, tested tools that incorporate research on overuse and underuse of care to identify the most "impactable" members. The analytic models uniquely incorporate local healthcare system factors and practice patterns, as well as patient receptivity to coaching intervention.

While the individual impacts of each of these components might be hard to tease out as is true for the individual components of any program, the synergy of their combination is easy to see.

What Do All the Examples in Chapters 5, 6, and 7 Have in Common?

Dan Quayle once said: "The role of the Vice President can be summed up in one word: to be prepared." Likewise, these examples can be summed up in one word: credibility that goes well beyond face validity, with promises and/or results that are not based on wishful thinking.

To create a successful program, eggs need to be broken. Sometimes this involves increasing co-pays on lifestyle drugs, as in the Alere example. Sometimes it requires redesigning your benefits and negotiating hard with your carrier, as in the Quantum example, and sometimes it calls for pestering people to go to the doctor, as in the Black Box example. In the case of the two health plans, it's treating your doctors like they matter. And sometimes it entails a serious resource commitment, as in the HealthDialog example.

Simple overlays and painless solutions don't work. In the immortal words of the great philosopher H. L. Mencken: "Every problem, no matter how complex, has a simple and easily understood answer. And it's almost always wrong."

I hadn't actually thought of the above as the unifying attribute of the previous three chapters until an e-mail for a webinar by a wellness vendor (Vendor O) popped into my inbox with the same metaphorical impact of the apple falling on Isaac Newton's head that inspired him to discover gravity, except that the former really happened.

The heading was: "How Health Plans and Employers Are Using HRAs to Help Transform Their Business [*sic*]." The webinar's producers promised that we would learn insights about HRAs that would make them "strategic tools for improved business performance."

Maybe that's true on Vendor O's planet, but if you ask the CEOs of earth's 100 most successful companies to name the 100 "strategic tools" they've focused on to "improve business performance" —a total of 10,000 data points—they will mention HRAs approximately zero times, about the same number of times that they cite neat handwriting. (Most CEOs in this hypothetical survey would also note that one way to improve business performance is not trying to "focus" on 100 ways to improve business performance.)

I've probably taken more HRAs than anyone in the country, and I can tell you that even with some follow-up coaching, they have little measurable value for employers, and certainly, to use the words of the webinar promoter, no "strategic, game-changing" value. Health plans have figured this out. Health plans have too much sense to think these are useful tools to reduce the medical costs of their insured populations in the short term. No HMO in the country—not a single one—pays fully insured members to take HRAs online. They simply sell HRAs to their self-insured employer customers, who for a variety of reasons (some good and some bad) find them to be a worthwhile expenditure.

The other thing I've learned from taking all these HRAs is that HRAs are all basically alike. You can infer that simply by how much time vendors spend trying to convince you that theirs is different. HRAs feed us back what we already know, albeit in slightly different ways: We need to quit smoking, eat better, exercise more, and get less stressed out. Offering HRAs is a classic case of H. L. Mencken's simple and easily understood answer.

What you need to make wellness and disease management successful is exactly the opposite: Spend your money not to pay people to take a survey, but rather to create a culture that makes your company such a pleasant and supportive and healthy place to work that people will want to work there.

Chapter 8

Contracting/RFP Checklist of Do's and Don'ts (Mostly Don'ts)

This final chapter will synthesize all the lessons so far—and then some—into a checklist. Reading this chapter is one way to learn how to write RFPs and vendor contracts.

Another way is to skip this chapter, study the 2011 to 2012 Commonwealth of Virginia RFP for disease management and wellness, and then do everything exactly the opposite way. For instance, here is the RFP's financial guarantee section in its entirety:

> Describe any guaranteed improvements in financial outcomes and return on investment and the amount of the fees at-risk for each year of the contract. You must include a description of the ROI methodology. Be sure to identify each component included in your ROI measures such as reduction in medical/Rx cost, cost of productivity, absenteeism, and presenteeism, etc. We understand that this may be a preliminary guarantee based upon demographics only and could change once you have analyzed historical claims experience.

If that guarantee section doesn't already appear comically wrong to you, look at it again after you read this chapter. This chapter draws on other examples, too, but nobody combines conciseness and cluelessness the way Virginia does. For instance, in the section of the RFP whose most critical attributes are precision, validity, and comparability, the last phrase you'd use is *et cetera*. Some might argue that the state drew their inspiration from "Eleanor," by the Turtles ("You're my pride and joy et cetera"). I, on the other hand, suspect that middle sentence was ghostwritten by Holden Caulfield, because so many commas are in the wrong places.*

Their pricing section is far too complex to reproduce here, so let's turn to the highlights reel. Consider the comparison below between the recommended combined pricing/guarantee template (provided later in this chapter) versus Virginia's pricing-only template that somehow must get reconciled with the earlier comma-intensive guarantee template:

Number of pricing cells in *Why Nobody Believes* template, *including* the guarantee section	10
Number of pricing cells in Virginia RFP, *in addition to* the guarantee section	231

The good news is that anyone with a job opening for a former state director of benefits is likely to have at least one candidate. I know what you're thinking, but, yes, I did notify him in advance, point out these flaws, and offer to remove this passage if he addressed these flaws—and, no, he elected to move forward as is (and don't think I'm not grateful for that). As Tina Rosenberg says in *Join the Club:* "No amount of information can budge us when we refuse to be budged."

Worst practices are more fun but best practices are more instructive, so apologies in advance if the rest of this chapter on contracting isn't very funny.

---

*This allusion is obscure even for *Why Nobody Believes,* but it was too *apropos* to pass up. In J. D. Salinger's *Catcher in the Rye,* Stradlater convinces Holden to write his English paper, but cautions: "That [teacher] thinks you're a hot-shot in English, and he knows you're my roommate. So don't stick all the commas in the right places."

Contractual clauses can be divided into three categories:

1. Those directly related to validity, meaning those that were covered in this book.
2. Those not specifically related to the numbers, but that facilitate or are related to valid contracting.
3. Those not related to the numbers at all.

The third category is why you have procurement officers and lawyers. They handle stuff like indemnification and assignment and conflict-of-laws and all those other clauses that no one ever reads except occasionally the people who write them. We won't be covering that category. We'll focus our energies on the first two categories, because this chapter is specifically designed to aid self-insured employers (and health plans that are outsourcing programs) in their contracting to avoid the pitfalls of invalidity.

Category 1: Clauses Designed Specifically for Validity

METHODOLOGY—COMPARISON GROUP

Do not accept any methodology that includes *any mention* of the following things:

1. **Inflation-adjusted trend**. That was disproven in Chapter 1.
2. **Using "projected cost" based on the "non-disease population" or "non-disease members" as a comparison**. Once again, disproven in Chapter 1.
3. **Any reference to the "Johns Hopkins Methodology"**, which even Johns Hopkins doesn't use any more because it is so obviously invalid, resembling the *prospective identification* methodology
4. **Measuring results on active participants only**. I thought everyone had stopped doing analysis this way (except the late-night comedy shows) until I saw this state employee RFP: "Confirm that your ROI data contains only members who are actively participating in a DM program. 'Actively

participating' excludes members who have been contacted by phone or mail but have not responded... ROIs that are not based on engaged and active participation [sic] of the member will be considered inaccurate and invalid." I've seen people insist on blatantly incorrect metrics before but never as adamantly as these guys. In fact, I've never seen anyone take a position on anything so clearly wrong with such career-ending conviction since Colin Powell revealed Iraq's weapons of mass destruction to the U.N. General Assembly.

5. **A requirement for "continuous enrollment" to qualify for being measured in the disease group**. Fact is, people who are not continuously enrolled spend differently. If they know they are about to be hired, they postpone spending until they are covered. If they think they are about to be fired (and COBRA uptake is not close to 100 percent), they squeeze in as much healthcare as possible. Worst case, they feign or overstate illness to qualify for disability. Also, you spend money on everyone. No reason that you shouldn't measure your savings against everyone.

6. **Measuring on only the high-cost members or worse, comparing the performance of the high-cost members to the other members**. A classic heads-and-tails.

METHODOLOGY—MEASURING ROI GENERALLY

1. **Tell. Don't ask.** "Describe how you calculate savings," and "What is your ROI?" are just begging for trouble. Let's revisit that very same State RFP, whose name I'm not mentioning simply because my cousin works for the state and while they can't fire me for observing that they should fire their consultant, they can fire him: "Describe your methodologies for calculating and reporting cost savings," and also, for some reason using Title Case (See How Funny Title Case Looks When You're Not Reading a Title?), "What Return on Investment Have You Experienced with Your Disease Management Programs?" Between these two questions and the insistence on measuring invalidly, rather than pay for the program with taxpayer money, the state might as well just

send its taxpayers the address for the winning vendor, with instructions on how to mail them the cash directly. Quite the contrary, you should *tell* the vendors the event reduction you want, using the event-based plausibility method of measuring outcomes, and have the vendors tell you how much various targets will cost. There is a display farther down (following the discussion of at-risk fees) that shows a sample of how this should look in an RFP.

2. **Measuring on the high-cost or high-risk members only**. "High-cost" refers to last year's high-cost members, who of course decline in cost as a group no matter what you do. "High-risk" members are basically high-cost members passed through some kind of "black box" (small *b*'s) screen that does little more than substitute the word "risk" for "cost". Either way, it is a classic heads-to-tails issue.

3. A corollary to that one: **Do not attempt in any way, shape, or form to try to divide populations by risk level.** The best example is the Washington State RFP for disease management. At 25,000 words, it was half as long as this book, and about 3,000 times as expensive. The consultants split the population into a head-spinning array of diseases (to ensure non-comparability and therefore create the need for more billable hours to do the invalid analysis, the consultants—Benefits Consulting Firm A, for a change—allowed the vendors to pick two of their own diseases in addition to the two required ones) and risk levels. News alert: Risk levels are completely transient and hence meaningless. It's not just heads-to-tails: With *four* risk levels (the number contemplated in the Washington RFP), coins would be flipping more than Bing Crosby's pennies from heaven.

4. **Anything that is measured on the "diseased members" or the "disease population" or "members with the disease", and so forth, is also classic heads-to-tails.** Washington, for example, attempted to do an ersatz plausibility analysis by asking for a year-over-year comparison of admit rates—but they then added "per 1,000 disease members," which of course defeats the point of a valid period-over-period comparison by adding—you guessed it—a heads-to-tails fallacy.

5. Speaking of which, **never just assume that because a vendor/carrier mentions "plausibility indicators" or "plausibility testing" that they intend to do actual valid plausibility tests.** Vendors cheat on plausibility tests, too. There is frequently a little asterisk, figuratively speaking. Recently, in a best-and-final-offer RFP, I insisted on measuring events across the population as a plausibility test. One vendor wrote: "Agreed. We will measure events on the entire known disease population, whether contacted or not." Of course, that is precisely the opposite of a plausibility test, which involves counting events in the entire *unknown* population, as well, not just the population already known to have the diagnosis, which would be measuring on "heads" only. Adding the word "Agreed" in front of the answer doesn't change the answer itself.

6. **Any mention of the CCA guidelines for outcomes measurement needs to be paired with a DYA or plausibility test.** And if not mentioned in the RFP, any mention of CCA guidelines in an RFP response needs the same in order to be valid.

7. **Never try to reconcile individual diseases to get ROIs for individual diseases**, a task whose only value is to enrich consultants. Ask anyone who works for the state of Washington how much fun that was.

8. **Never let a vendor offer a guarantee and then have the option to change it after they review the claims following the award**, like Virginia did. You will certainly be hit with the four words you least want to hear from a vendor after the award is made: "Oh, by the way." Nothing good in this industry has ever come out of a sentence starting "Oh, by the way." Instead, *tell* vendors what your event rates are in advance, using the ICD-9 table from Chapter 2. If you can't spend 10 minutes to do that event rate analysis, estimate the event rates and set up a formula for automatic guarantee adjustment if your estimate is wrong. If the events turn out to be lower (and hence reducing the number of them harder), the guarantee can be formulaically diminished and vice-versa.

CLAUSES SPECIFIC TO WELLNESS MEASUREMENT

Financial Outcomes   Most wellness financial outcomes measurements are wrong. For wellness to reduce healthcare expenses, there must be reductions in the (a) system-wide claims (b) theoretically reducible by wellness. Those claims "theoretically reducible by wellness" are pretty much the same as the events for disease management, plus possibly rates of non-trauma ER visits, specialist referrals, and bariatric surgeries.

But those latter categories are long shots, and in general, I find the events affected by wellness and disease management to be so similar that if an organization has both wellness and disease management in place, I often tell clients that it's impossible to split out the effects of each unless one program simply had a much lower participation rate than the other relative to the eligibility pool.

Pay careful attention to this paragraph because this sums up why even if there are other ways in which wellness reduces claims cost, contracts should highlight event rates. Suppose wellness could reduce the utilization of many different resources. Some wellness promoters will say it can reduce the cost of anything. But surely it reduces events, like heart attacks, that are more directly related to diet and exercise than events like train wrecks that aren't, right? So why not make a list of the events most likely to decline and say that a claimed overall cost reduction is invalid if the events most likely to contribute positively to that cost reduction don't decline by at least as much as the alleged average?

You might even ask, "Why isn't there a list of wellness plausibility indicators in this book?" Remarkably, unlike in disease management, no one has ever attempted to track the sources of wellness savings to create plausibility indicators. People are happy enough to say: "The savings could come from anywhere," which allows vendors and carriers to combine the Greatest Hits of Fallacies (participants versus non-participants, inflation trending, high-risk members only) into a savings percentage with no plausibility check to prevent them.

For our part, we are happy enough just to see an *a priori* list of ICD-9s and procedures more likely to decline than others. Any list. We just want to see that someone has thought of this. Wellness is probably a multibillion-dollar industry by now, and—in addition to no one knowing how big it is—no one knows or has even guessed *where* they save this massive amount of money that vendors claim to be saving.

Productivity Improvements   In addition to the slight likelihood that medical claims may fall, wellness may increase productivity in two ways. One way, presenteeism—the concept of being at work but not being focused—is very difficult to measure. This is not just because these days most people don't have jobs whose output can be objectively measured, but also because there are so many other things not related to wellness that impact presenteeism, like the NCAA pool.

Fortunately, the good news is that the other way that productivity can be improved, reduced absenteeism, can be measured. Further, absenteeism presumably correlates with presenteeism, besides being quite expensive on its own, as absent workers draw a salary anyway and often need substitutes. Simply summing up and comparing total workplace absences (not absences just for the people offered the program because their absence rate was high) before and after a program would be an excellent contractual term in an absence management program. Since this is so obvious a way to measure absences and since so many organizations implement absence management or wellness programs with an absence management component, it's barely even worth taking up space to mention this as a necessary clause for a contract.

Except that no one ever puts that clause in.

Why not? For starters, shockingly few organizations even measure their absence rates. About a decade ago, most organizations switched to a system in which employees got a certain amount of paid time off, or PTO, that they could use for sick days, personal days, or vacation. The idea was that by assigning a "price" to a sick day as being the same as a vacation day, people would take fewer sick days. Though no doubt a good management incentive for that reason, PTO complicates the measurement of absence days.

The consequence: Vendors get to measure absences however they want to, which naturally means invalidly. The poster children in Chapter 3 take full advantage of that, claiming savings in excess of 100 percent in their absence management programs.

The classic absenteeism and presenteeism measurement is to simply survey people and ask them respectively whether, as compared to last year, they took more days off or were feeling less productive at work. That's squishy enough, but normally vendors survey only the people who completed the coaching, meaning people (1) whose risk scores were high enough to qualify for coaching *and* (2) who elected to participate in coaching *and* (3) who the vendor coached successfully enough that they were happy to complete the survey. Let me see, hmm... that's a heads-or-tails fallacy plus two self-selection fallacies—an invalidity trifecta. Hence, do not allow this type of measurement in your contract.

Going a step further, my recommendation is simply not to undertake a program if you can't collect the information needed to determine if it works. Absence measurement is Exhibit A for that recommendation—no sense paying people to manage it if you can't measure the results. However, if you are willing to do the measurement work, absences are a tangible and intuitive measure of productivity. There are also a few excellent self-reported productivity tools available. Sean Sullivan, whose Institute for Health and Productivity Management probably does more of this work than anyone, recommends Debra Lerner's Work Limitation Questionnaire. We would add, try to combine any self-reported productivity tool with non-self-reported absence data. If both trend together, each confirms the other.

Risk Reduction Whatever else your wellness program accomplishes, it should reduce risk factors. Not risk factors on the coached population, or the participating population, or the high-risk population, or on any other fraction of the population, but on virtually the whole population. Fairly mandatory or heavily incentivized biometric screens are the preferred method for this comparison.

Category 2: Clauses That Are Not Specifically Related to Metrics Validity but That Unfortunately Fit the Oscar Wilde Observation, "Experience Is the Name You Give to Your Mistakes."

ADMINISTRATIVE FEE BREAKOUT

Many employers still fail to anticipate in their carrier RFPs and contracts that they might want to carve out certain components of that contract/administrative fee down the road. You might think, "Well, we would never forget that clause," but I've found only two contracts that fully anticipate this possibility. Often, there is broad language allowing carve-outs, but I'm referring to contracts in which every component of the administrative fee was priced separately with an explicit provision that the customer could carve out whichever component(s) they wanted to at any future point. (In all fairness, the carrier in both cases charged a fee to do this, but a modest and clearly defined one.)

Absent this clause anticipating the discussion, it is much more difficult to negotiate a carve-out down the road. If not addressed in the contract, the carrier will respond to a disease management carve-out request with one or two of the following canards:

1. They can't break out their administrative fee, so if you want to do disease management separately through an independent vendor, you will have to do it as an add-on, with no reduction in the administrative fee.

2. Their disease management costs only [insert a random small amount], so you are welcome to carve it out separately, but they will be reducing the administrative fee only by that same random small amount.

3. You are welcome to outsource the program to an independent vendor and there will be a small reduction in their administrative fee, but there is also a fee of [insert a random large amount] associated with the coordination with an outside vendor.

Further, if you intend to consider a more comprehensive out-source than "straight" disease management—like a Quantum Health-type program—which requires carving out member services and/or other administrative functions, you can kiss that option goodbye if you haven't already anticipated the possibility of doing this in your carrier contract. Otherwise, there is no way health plans willingly agree to carving out member services, a large chunk of what they do. As one (not surprisingly, male) carrier executive put it to me: "That would be like getting married and then allowing your wife to carve out the sex."

FEES, CONTRACT LENGTH, AND TERMINATION REQUIREMENTS

As a buyer, you should be willing to be flexible on the term of the PHI contract because a longer-term contract will generally contain a lower price with the exception noted in the next paragraph. On the other hand, you should be adamant about the not-for-cause termination clause, which basically gives you the right to walk away if the vendors start playing with the outcomes numbers (or doing anything else untoward). The true length of the contract is really governed by the formula: Number of months before not-for-cause termination notice can be given plus number of months' notice needed before terminating. So, a five-year contract that allows six months' notice to be given at any point after 18 months is really a two-year contract followed by ongoing six-month extensions, which gives the buyer more leverage when issues arise.

The exception: Never agree to fee increases indexed to inflation. Fees for population health management rarely if ever increase. You are not doing yourselves a favor by locking in an inflation adjustment that over time increases to a level well in excess of what new contracts are priced at. A flat-rate multiyear fee is much preferred.

Next, speaking of fees, one classic question is: "Should we price per member per month (PMPM) or per case per month (PCPM)?" The difference is whether the fees are spread over everyone or whether the fees are concentrated only amongst the disease population. The general answer is to choose PMPM. Not that PMPM is a panacea for all that ails mankind, but PCPM is fraught with peril. First, the definition of "case" can be squishy. The more members/employees get defined as diseased, the greater the overall fees. This is *especially* true for patient-centered medical homes, in which (in some models) extra fees are paid only on chronically ill patients. There are patients who are obviously sick, patients who are obviously healthy, and a ton in between. As Oliver Wendell Holmes* once said: "Somewhere between night and day, a fine line has to be drawn." Give doctors (in the case of PCMH) or vendors (in DM) an opportunity to put people in a category that nets them more money, and more people will show up in that category. Funny how that happens.

Related to that, there are several other money pits for per-case pricing:

1. As mentioned, **never, ever agree to pay a fee that varies according to the risk category of the patient.** Risk categories are not etched in stone and there is nothing about them that is objective. Offer to pay by risk category and watch how many patients get into the high-risk category. There is a way to address that, which is by setting up maximums for each risk category. But going through that effort yields basically the same PCPM as a simple one-size-fits-all PCPM price.

2. **Be extremely clear about how much disease manager contact is required for someone to remain in the per-case payment category**, before they get switched to a much lower maintenance payment level, when/whether they "graduate" from per-case pricing, and how many months a non-graduated member can go without contact before the vendor stops charging for them.

3. **Per-case has to be opt-in rather than opt-out**, or you'll end up paying monthly per-case fees for people who, figuratively speaking, wouldn't be able to pick their disease managers

---

*Ironically, Holmes is the only person we have quoted so far in *Why Nobody Believes* who is not referred to as an "immortal philosopher" and yet he would arguably have a stronger claim to that appellation than Yogi Berra, Ned Flanders, and Rick Perry combined.

out of a police lineup. (And given the way they measure, it wouldn't surprise me if some of them ended up in one.)

RISK-BASED PRICING AND GUARANTEES

Risk-based pricing clauses based on ROI are generally the worst-negotiated clauses by the buyer's consultants in a contract, a difficult superlative to achieve given the number of other poorly negotiated clauses. As mentioned earlier, the classics, "What has your ROI experience been?" and "Tell us how you calculate ROI" should have become obsolete by now, joining mood rings, hot pants, and liberal Republicans. Many trees have been sacrificed in order to make these clauses as complex and invalid as possible, with consultants and vendors equally at fault.

George Bernard Shaw once started a letter, allegedly to Winston Churchill: "Dear Winston, Sorry this letter is so long. I didn't have time to make it short."

The good news is I have had time—16 years in this field, to be exact—to make it short. As a result, 80 percent of what you need to know about both risk-based pricing and outcomes-based performance guarantees can be found in this one display. Start with valid event rate-based metrics, provide the vendors with blanks to complete and the ICD-9s you'll be measuring, give them 0 percent-to-100 percent risk (or some other maximum risk) and then you'll get valid and comparable bids.

Four-condition PMPM fees (constant for three years) at the following event rate reduction levels and guarantees:

	3%	5%	7%	Other (Specify)
100% fees at risk	☐	☐	☐	☐
0% fees at risk	☐	☐	☐	☐

(continued)

(continued)

Additional amount to be added to your bid if you provide the savings calculations [   ]

High-risk asthma *opt-in* program, per phone call or per month[*] [   ]

*Specify which—do not add marketing expense

Things to note:

1. Each year's bid is held constant to prevent the inflation ratcheting discussed earlier.
2. I always add an "other-specify" column so as not to overly constrain the bidders.
3. There is no point in paying vendors to provide the actuarial savings calculations when they are going to reconcile invalidly anyway. This line will show you how much that costs. Instead of, paying them to make up numbers, simply apply a cost figure to the average avoided event, count the avoided events, and multiply. This approach is much cheaper than whatever they would do, and in the immortal words of the great philosopher Henry Kissinger, has the additional virtue of being the truth, keeping in mind that "whole patient" management would also find some savings in co-morbidities that can be estimated via the co-morbidity multipliers laid out in Chapter 2.
4. In disease management, never contract for asthma except on a high-risk, opt-in basis. The numbers simply don't add up for most asthmatics. It costs much more to manage a patient than to take the risk that once every few years he or she might need an ER visit. Hence the optional asthma exclusion.
5. The actual price in this grid will vary according to the percentages of fees placed at risk by the vendor, as well as the event rate inflection promised. During the contracting process, you can interpolate amongst the completed cells to come up with what you want for a risk/price combination.

PREPARING FOR THE END OF THE CONTRACT

Here are four classic mistakes to avoid during the contracting process concerning the end of the contractual period:

1. **Avoid automatic renewal**. Oftentimes, a buyer allows a vendor to add a clause that says if notice is not given at least ·90/180 (or whatever) days before the end of a contract, it automatically renews for another year. If you've added the not-for-cause termination clause, this should be a non-issue. Nonetheless, don't lock yourself into a renewal or long-term extension if you miss a deadline. Instead, put in a simple at-will extension.

2. **Speaking of extensions, the pricing terms should be extended if the contract is extended**. There shouldn't be any "automatic reversion" to anything.

3. **You should anticipate that there will be a handoff to the next vendor** and require that the current vendor return all contact/member information to you (if you are a health plan) or a designated HIPAA-compliant entity (if you are an employer and are not allowed to see employee information).

4. If you are a health plan, **make sure that after termination the vendor is not allowed to solicit your joint customers** without your express advance permission. Ask Blue Cross of Minnesota about this one.

THE 24/7 INBOUND COMPONENT OF THE CONTRACT

Increasingly, the 24/7 inbound triage nurseline is being incorporated into the DM or PHI contract. Almost invariably, pricing for this service is done on a PMPM basis, and equally almost invariably nobody does the math to see if the number of calls remotely fills the PMPM assumption for usage. I've seen one situation where it quite literally would have been cheaper to simply send all callers to the ER than to actually answer the phone. The PMPM fee/number of expected or actual calls should be less than $30/call, as opposed to the $150 or more that people pay if they don't do the math.

DISPUTE RESOLUTION

The major source of disputes is over whether the vendor "hits their numbers" according to the terms of their risk-based pricing. If you follow the guidelines above, there should never be a dispute over this because the guidelines are so transparent. Nonetheless, just in case, we would recommend reserving the right to revert to the non-risk-based price, retrospectively to the beginning of the reconciliation period, if you can't agree on what ROI was achieved. Why pay them a risk premium if they aren't willing to refund your money if they miss your target?

Appendix: The Keys to the Numerical Kingdom

In this book, we've shown you how an application of common sense can help you determine whether or not (usually the "or not" option) an outcome is real. However, there are certain factoids you also need to have in your head (or keep this page around) to be able to judge validity.

First, you need to know how much you spend, on which resources. There are no hard-and-fast figures for these percentages, but there are rules of thumb. Plausibility is all about rules of thumb, because precision and accuracy are often inversely related in this field. (For instance, if I see a reported ROI with more than one digit to the right of the decimal point, I automatically know the whole report is wrong because anyone who understands ROI knows you can't calculate one with two-decimal-point precision.)

With that in mind, figure that, for the commercially insured, <65 population:

Category	Range of Your Spending Percentage
Inpatient—ambulatory-care sensitive	12%–18%
Inpatient—birth events (including neonate)	10%–15%
Inpatient—other	15%–25%
Outpatient	18%–24%
ER	3%–5%
Other ancillary	9%–12%
Pharmaceuticals	18%–26%

Of course, these proportions will vary by condition, severity, and how these categories are grouped and reported. For instance, an older population with a higher illness burden will incur a higher proportion of inpatient costs.

Next, your program—whether disease management, wellness, or patient-centered medical home—is attempting to reduce utilization. To reduce utilization, you need to know, well, your utilization. If you guessed that I am about to say, "Remarkably, most people don't know their utilization rates and neither do their consultants," you've been paying some attention lo these many pages. Let us solve this mystery for you.

Like EPA mileage estimates, your utilization may vary, in this case probably +/−20 percent, but the range is accurate in the commercially insured, <65 population:

Category	Units of Utilization per 1,000 Covered Lives
Admissions	62
Days	250
ER visits	160
Doctor visits	4000
Heart attacks	1
Total admissions/1,000 for the 5 inpatient common chronic condition categories, primary-coded	9

One insight from these tables: There are some obvious physical limitations to the amount of event reduction and resource use reduction that can be claimed through any program, because there aren't that many avoidable admissions and reducible resources. However, many of the case studies don't seem at all constrained by those limitations. For instance, for the numbers to add up, the North Carolina and Vendor M studies would have to eliminate all the avoidable admissions as well as a noticeable chunk of the *nonavoidable* admissions, not just for the participants but for most of their families, friends, and casual acquaintances.

Author's Note on Sources

Obviously, one cannot "blind" vendors and still provide sources, right? That would be like when Casey Stengel instructed his players to "line up alphabetically by height." There are slight changes to many of the displays and quotes for which the originators—mind you, *all people who have spent the past several years trying to get as much exposure as possible for these displays and quotes*—would not give permission to be displayed or quoted. Absent permission, changes are important for copyright protection (meaning "are important to keep me from getting sued"). None of these changes alter the points being made, though. The good news is that copyrights protect only the expression of clueless ideas, not the clueless ideas themselves.

A source document, which includes missing citations and most of the vendor names, is available directly from the Disease Management Purchasing Consortium website. In a thesaurus, of course, "available" is not synonymous with "free." You do need to go to www.dismgmt.com and follow the link to PayPal. Once you pay your $29, these secrets of the universe will download into your inbox.

Notes

Chapter 1   Actuaries Behaving Badly

1. Ariel Linden and Steven Goldberg, "The Case-Mix of Chronic Illness Hospitalization Rates in a Managed Care Population: Implications for Health Management Programmes," *Journal of Evaluation in Clinical Practice* 13, no. 6 (2007): 947–951.

2. *CCA Outcomes Guidelines,* 73.

3. Iver Juster, Steven Rosenberg, Deeptimayee Senapati, and Mayur Shah, "'Dial-an-ROI?' Changing Basic Variables Impacts Cost Trends in Single-Population Pre-Post (CCA Type) Saving Analysis." *Population Health Improvement* 12, no. 1 (2009): 17–24.

Chapter 3   Case Studies That Flunk Every Plausibility Test Known to Mankind

1. See press advisory from the Georgia Attorney General's office, February 22, 2011, http://law.ga.gov/00/press/detail/0,2668,87670814_87670929_168474870,00.html.

2. Ariel Linden, "Estimating the Effect of Regression to the Mean in Health Management Programs," Wolters Kluwer Health | Adis, *Disease Management and Health Outcomes* 15, no. 1 (2007): 7–12.

Chapter 4   Case Studies That Flunk Every Plausibility Test Known to Mankind and Then Some

1. *The 10th Annual (2012) Report on the Disease Management and Wellness Industries* estimates both industries to combine to roughly $6 billion in economic activity, www.dismgmt.com/best-plans.

2. See Katherine Baicker, David Cutler, and Zirui Song, "Workplace Wellness Programs Can Generate Savings," *Health Affairs* 29, no. 2 (February 2010), for a meta-analysis of these programs.

3. This "natural flow of risk" slide can be easily found online. For example, at http://www.welcoa.org/freeresources/pdf/Edington_INTERVIEW_1.pdf.

4. Barbara Naydeck, Janine Pearson, Ronald Ozminkowski, Brian Day, and Ron Goetzel, "The Impact of the Highmark Employee Wellness Programs on 4-Year Healthcare Costs," *Journal of Occupational and Environmental Medicine* 50, no. 2 (February 2008): 146 ff.

5. Katherine Baicker, David Cutler, and Zirui Song, "Workplace Wellness Programs Can Generate Savings," *Health Affairs* 29, no. 2 (February 2010): 2.

6. http://hcupnet.ahrq.gov/HCUPnet.jsp.

7. www.cdc.gov/tobacco/data_statistics/state_data/state_highlights/2010/pdfs/highlights2010.pdf.

8. www.cdc.gov/obesity/data/trends.html#State.

9. www.kff.org/medicaid/upload/8136.pdf.

10. "Joint Principles of the Patient-Centered Medical Home,"American Academy of Family Physicians, American Academy of Pediatrics, American College of Physicians, and American Osteopathic Association, March 2007.

11. Patient-Centered Medical Home Performance Metrics for Employers, www.pcpcc.net.

12. Ibid., 21.

13. Leading Disease Management Organizations, *9th Annual Report on the Disease Management and Wellness Industries*, Health Industries Research Companies, 2010, 17.

14. www.ncmedsoc.org/non_members/legislative/ac/ACO-CCNC-Dobson.pdf.

15. Study available from author alewis@dismgmt.com.

16. Disease Management Blog, February 5, 2009, http://diseasemanagementcareblog.blogspot.com/2009/02/community-care-of-north-carolina.html.

17. "NC Program a Model for Health Overhaul?" *Morning Edition*, October 15, 2009.

18. Community Care of North Carolina: "Putting Health Reform Ideas into Practice in Medicaid, Health Plan H Commission on Medicaid and the Uninsured," May 2009.

19. Centers for Disease Control and Prevention, Maps of Diabetes and Obesity, 1994, 2000, and 2009, September 2010, www.cdc.gov/diabetes/statistics/slides/maps_diabetesobesity94.pdf.

20. www.communitycarenc.com.

21. Louisiana Department of Health and Hospitals Facts, January 10, 2011.

22. Seth Serxner, Soeren Mattke, Sarah Zakowski, and D. Gold, "Testing the CCA's Recommendations for Program Evaluation," *Population Health Improvement* 11, no. 5 (2008): 245.

23. www.communitycarenc.com.

24. The Commonwealth Fund. http://www.commonwealthfund.org/Publications/Issue-Briefs/2011/Nov/State-Trends-in-Premiums.aspx.

25. www.healthcareitnews.com/news/north-carolina-takes-medicaid-pilot-private-sector.

26. www.ncmedsoc.org/non_members/legislative/ac/ACO-CCNC-Dobson.pdf, 6.

27. Critical Outcomes Report Analysis training and certification, Disease Management Purchasing Consortium, www.dismgmt.com/certs/cora/self-study.

28. American Diabetes Association, "Economic Costs of Diabetes in the US in 2002," *Diabetes Care* 26, no. 3 (2003): 917–932.

29. Citation available from author.

Chapter 7   Disease Management Programs That Actually Work (Pinch Me)

1. www.fiercehealthcare.com/story/study-medicare-disease-management-pilot-failed/2009–02–11.

Glossary

The following definitions describe the terms used in *Why Nobody Believes the Numbers* to describe the services that you may be contracting for, and/or services that someone is going to try to sell you, or terms that salespeople use during the sales process.

Biometric screening is an objective tool whereby people are tested for various risk factors, often at a health fair. Occasionally, such screens reveal people at high risk who did not know they were at high risk. Assuming you stick with basic parameters, biometric screening on an entire population may be the most valuable aspect of a wellness program for both identification and risk measurement. (Not that there is much competition for either distinction.) Of course, your costs will rise as a result of taking the necessary preventive measures on patients revealed as high-risk by the biometric screen—one more reason why it is not possible to achieve savings in wellness in the first year—but these preventive measures will help you avoid debilitating events down the road.

Care Continuum Alliance (CCA). Formerly the Disease Management Association of America (and now www.CareContinuum .org), the CCA publishes guidelines (available free for download) that, being consensus-based instead of math-based, say pretty much the opposite of what this book says, and two of the examples of math that doesn't add up were drawn from presentations given at their 2010 annual forum. (The 2011 forum had its share, too. Those North Carolina Medicaid people simply won't shut up.) We don't pick on them because they are particularly faulty—there is actually a lot of excellent material on them if one overlooks the pre-post premise arithmetic *faux pas*. ("Aside from that, how did you enjoy the theater, Mrs. Lincoln?") We pick on them because, as inveterate gambler William "Canada Bill" Jones replied when informed that a particular card game was crooked: "Yes, but it's the only game in town." Yup, that's where the expression originated.

Care management is a catchall term that doesn't really mean anything, specifically. It can be disease management alone, or it can be Population Health Improvement, or anything in between. (This category would normally not include wellness. You have to have something wrong with you to qualify for a care management program.) Any initiative done on behalf of a payor that directly touches a member—whether a health plan or a self-insured employer—that is not paid for by a claims submission and that does not require a co-pay or a provider visit, and is not wellness, would fall into this category.

Case management means two very different things, depending on whether you are a case manager or a disease manager. A traditional case manager's role is to facilitate discharge from an acute care setting by ensuring that the patient is provided with whatever he or she needs to continue convalescing at a lower level of care. That type of case management rarely includes educating people on long-term management of their condition via the telephone. Conversely, ask a disease manager what constitutes case management, and he or (more likely) she will say exactly that: education on self-management, with tools and backup support.

CCA Guidelines. See Care Continuum Alliance.

Disease management is briefly definable as "the eyes and ears of the practicing physician between visits," and best described not by a dry definition but rather by a vignette. How many times has the following happened to you: You seek medical care for a complaint. The doctor describes what's going on, gives you a prescription, and tells you what to do. You ask some questions and then leave. On your way out the door, you suddenly remember a question or two you forgot to ask, and/or you forgot one of the doctor's answers. Not a big deal. Whatever you have will almost certainly get better on its own anyway if you take the pills, and probably even if you don't. Now, re-consider that situation, except that this time, instead of being you, you are 40 years older, have multiple issues, are taking many drugs, and maybe are a bit forgetful. For someone in this position, unaddressed questions and forgotten answers can be health-threatening and may result in a trip to the ER. That's why shortly (shortly, at least, in theory) after that doctor visit and then consistently thereafter, someone calls you to make sure that kind of emergency doesn't arise by answering all of your questions and providing helpful advice.

Dummy year analysis or dummy year adjustment (DYA) is a check on what happens if you just apply an outcomes methodology to a cohort's numbers without actually doing anything to the people in the cohort. If you start out with a group that is high cost, high utilizing, or high risk (whether risk scores are based on previous claims patterns or HRA results), that group will decline in cost/utilization/risk the next year absent any intervention. Taking this so-called "regression to the mean" into account when measuring outcomes constitutes a DYA. Few vendors propose a DYA because it has a nasty habit of negating most of their alleged savings, leaving only a smidgen attributable to the actual intervention. Hence the popularity of the current pre-post guidelines, which combine the actual savings plus the savings mirage created by regression to the mean, and then compare the resulting figure to a big fat non-chronic trend, to create a bottom line high enough to keep us all employed.

Gaps in care analysis is a matching of people's conditions to their drug therapy to try to find opportunities to improve therapies. These are well received in the marketplace because they sound very tangible. However, there are four problems with them. First, the information behind the care gaps is often outdated, leading one practitioner to tell a health plan medical director: "You realize that if your information was accurate my patient would be dead by now." Second, unlike the shockingly and probably inadvertently candid and valid vendor-generated example in this book, vendors often conveniently forget to offset gaps that close with gaps that open—a classic heads-to-tails fallacy. Third, a very large proportion of the gaps can be almost irrelevant from a medical economics viewpoint. Finally, the projected savings are never plausibility-tested and frequently exceed the theoretically avoidable savings through utilization reduction.

Health risk assessments (HRAs) ask you perhaps 30 to 100 questions about your health status and habits, and then, either instantly online or in the mail if you took a paper version of the assessment, give you interesting insights/advice about how to improve your health habits. For instance, if you say that you drive without a seat belt, their advice might possibly be to drive *with* a seat belt. Virtually every wellness vendor will tell you: "Our health risk assessment is unique/better because..." The fact is—and I say this having taken at least 15 of them—they are all pretty similar.

Medication therapy management (MTM) or chronic disease therapy management is a variation on disease management in which members are selected for the program based on the number of drugs they are taking. MTM is yet another intervention based on counting only the heads-to-tails members: The number of members whose pharmacy expense declines is not offset by the members whose pharmacy expense increases but who were not identified for the program originally because they were not taking enough drugs. As with everything else, this is not to say that MTM doesn't have value, but rather that the value could easily be substantially overstated.

Patient-centered medical homes are defined as "an approach to providing comprehensive primary care ... that facilitates partnerships between individual patients and their personal providers and, when appropriate, the patient's family."* PCMH advocates believe that increasing people's access to a heavily subsidized good (point-of-service healthcare) will somehow make people better off because as far as health is concerned, going to the doctor more is better. If this sounds familiar, it's because the same logic led to federal subsidized mortgages. Advocates felt that as far as home ownership was concerned, more would be better. PCMH may or may not work, but I am a bit skeptical of any intervention which the trade association's publication, *Family Practice Management* (11/09), advises physicians to initiate by billing the insurers up to $75,000 more/year for services they already provide.

---

*"Joint principles of the patient-centered medical home," American Academy of Family Physicians, American Academy of Pediatrics, American College of Physicians, and American Osteopathic Association, March 2007.

Population health improvement (PHI), sometimes called population health management, is the sum total of all the health-enhancing or disease-reducing services offered by a plan sponsor. A PHI strategy includes some or all of the other terms in this Glossary. Its goal is to reduce medical expenses, and increase productivity and morale, for your covered members (if a health plan) or employees plus dependents (if a self-insured employer). Broadly, any program in which you are asked to exchange "hard" dollars—that is, cash—for a "soft" payback in outcomes that are difficult to measure is a PHI program. If you want it described a bit less cynically, there is a definition-by-committee on the Care Continuum website.

Predictive modeling attempts to forecast future high utilizers based on current utilization patterns. You will often hear that such-and-such vendor was able to save money "versus predicted costs." If you've read this far into the book, your first reaction to the previous sentence would be: "How can anyone predict whether someone is going to get sick in the future based on a list of their insurance claims they incurred at least two months ago?" Your first reaction would be a good reaction. If your own doctor can't tell whether you are going to have a heart attack with anything approaching certainty, how can a vendor do that just by looking at your claims? However, a few organizations incorporate data beyond claims into their modeling, such as biometric screening or lab results. For them, predictive modeling will have value.

Return on investment (ROI) is defined as gross savings/fees, or in the case of internal programs, gross savings/cost. It's not just that gross savings are almost invariably measured wrong. The irony is—even if savings are measured right—ROI isn't the right way to look at impact. Ideally, you want to save the most money possible. If you invest $1 and save $10, your ROI is 10:1 and you've saved $9. If you invest $50 and save $100, your ROI is only 2:1 but you've saved $50. At the end of the year, your shareholders have more money. That's what counts, because corporations are people, too, you know.

Validation is the assertion that someone in authority has reviewed the methodology/outcomes/HRA and determined that it is somehow "valid." Just like a restaurant that promises "fine gourmet dining," the simple use of the phrase "validated outcomes" usually means the opposite.* I would know. I am one of the people who write these validation letters. Hey, you're not the only one with bills to pay. Usually the vendor who asks me is following standard industry practice and wants their customer to be assured of that. The vendor knows, and obviously I know, that standard industry practice is invalid, but those guidelines usually show savings. So my "validation" would be to say that the methodology is in compliance with standard industry practice, assuming it is. (Note: In those situations, I never say that the outcomes are actually valid, just that they are in compliance with industry guidelines. I am also often asked—usually by a buyer, not a seller—to validate whether an outcome is truly valid, and I do that, too.) The lesson for the buyers is to actually read validation letters paid for by a seller carefully, whether mine or anyone else's. For instance, Consulting Company C has written a letter for a vendor in which they "validate" the results but then say at the end: "We aren't validating the methodology, just the calculations."

Wellness is the attempt to maintain or improve the health of an entire population regardless of current health status, although some wellness programs exempt people who are already in disease management. Wellness is done primarily through health risk assessments, telephonic coaching (for people at high risk who are willing to participate in coaching), incentives, health fairs that often include biometric screening, and health education, usually online. The categories covered in wellness, especially wellness coaching, most often include smoking cessation and weight control. Other categories include fitness training, stress management, nutrition counseling, and so forth.

---

*Sometimes even validation doesn't do a vendor's results justice. For instance, Vendor A's outcomes, according to its website, aren't just validated. Nosirree! Regular validation is for sissies! Real Men, like Vendor A, get "strongly validated." Tough to be more validated than that. And what better way to end a book called *Why Nobody Believes the Numbers* than to answer the implied question in the title: Vendor A holds the record not just for the most "strongly validated" results, but also for the largest gap (85 percent) between marketing claims (85 percent cost reduction) and peer-reviewed findings (0 percent reduction).

About the Author

S earch on the phrase "invented disease management" and you will get Al Lewis. Mr. Lewis was also founder and first president of the Disease Management Association of America, now the Care Continuum Alliance. His Critical Outcomes Report Analysis certification, the only credential specifically devoted to population health management outcomes analysis, has been earned by about 200 people, while his Savings Measurement Validity certification has been bestowed upon roughly 30 health plans, employers, and states.

He provides procurement and outcomes consulting to health plans through www.dismgmt.com, the Disease Management Purchasing Consortium, and to employer human resource departments through www.hchc-consortium.com, the Health Care and Human Capital Consortium.

His two previous books, most recently *Disease Management and Wellness in the Post-Reform Era*, are the century's bestselling books on this admittedly rather narrow topic, while James Carville said the original economic policy ideas in his third book *Why the Heck Aren't We Already Doing This Stuff?* were presented with "humor and clarity, and with short enough words that even the densest presidential hopeful could understand them."

His background includes years as a partner in the international consulting firm of Bain & Company, while he has also run several healthcare companies, including one that didn't go bankrupt. He was called "the national leader in analyzing care management outcomes reports" by the *9th Annual Report on the Disease Management and Wellness Industries,* which he didn't even write. Plus, you can google him until both of you are blue in the face and you won't find any priors.

But he still can't get his kids to clean up their rooms.

Bibliography and Further Reading

I f you think the analysis in this book is rigorous but the prose isn't clever, then I would recommend something by Dave Barry. He is much cleverer than I am.

If you think the prose in this book is clever, but the analysis isn't rigorous, then I would recommend something by Ron Goetzel or Ariel Linden. Their analysis is much more rigorous than mine is.

If you think the prose isn't clever and the analysis isn't rigorous, then I would recommend not telling anyone.

Acknowledgments

To paraphrase the immortal words of the great philosopher Yogi Berra, I'd like to thank everyone who made this book necessary. Those would be the vendors, carriers, consultants, states, and associations whose executives never got the memo that you can't reduce a number by more than 100 percent. They provided me with the material, and I hope their soon-to-be-former customers and prospects will provide me with a ready market for this book.

Transitioning from good material to a book that can reach that ready market requires a lot of support from family and friends. Or at least that's the cliché. In fact, writing *Why Nobody Believes* required almost no support from anybody. You're always reading in acknowledgments how family and friends encouraged the project, helped the author overcome writer's block, persuaded the author not to abandon the book when it wasn't going well, pored over the manuscript making brilliant editorial suggestions, turned off the engine during the author's suicide attempt, and so on.

Well, my family has lives, and people who just finished reading *Why Nobody Believes* won't be surprised to learn I don't have any friends. Fortunately, with editors like Adrianna Johnson and Linda Indig and a publisher like Wiley, I don't need any. Everyone at Wiley was terrific.

There were some others. Scott Breidbart, who pointed out that "Bad money drives out good," is Gresham's Law, not Say's Law. (I was probably the only person ever to teach economics at Harvard not to know that.)

Ariel Linden. *Why Nobody Believes* mentions several times that math is not a popularity contest, it's proof-based, not consensus-based, and so on. All that is true, but even so it's a relief that a guy this smart agrees with me on the basic premise, even if he thinks I'm "still too soft on crime."

Alex Howlett, Vik Kudesia, and Jenkin Lee. Every standalone guy needs a webkid or two or three, to do everything from updating his site to backing his data up into the clouds (or something like that), all the time wondering not just how this old geezer can possibly make a living without being able to do this basic stuff but also how his ancestors even managed to learn to walk upright. Hey, it's a generational thing. What can I tell ya? My aunt doesn't even have email.

And while we're on the subject of people who know more about technology than I do, there's Tammy Rao, whose magical keyboard transformed humorous websites into equally humorous website reproductions that don't violate copyrights.

Now, here is a list of other people. I know you're thinking, oh, this is a humor book, so this is a set-up: Al's list is going to be comprised of fake people with funny names with double entendres, like Charles Ulmer Farley in *National Lampoon's High School Yearbook.* Or real people with funny names who didn't help with the book but did something to give Al an excuse to list their funny names, like the guys who invented television in order to keep vendors from doing their fifth-grade math homework (Philo T. Farnsworth, Vladimir Zworykin).

Unfortunately, these are (1) real people with (2) boring names. Peter Grant, David Nash, Sean Sullivan, Marc Perlman, Nicole Garrett, Dave Rearick, John Irvine, Pat Salber, Raymond Carter, Barbara Maxwell, Anne Llewellyn, Brian Klepper, Tobin Sharp, and John Marcille, all of whom have provided forums for my data-driven rants despite (in some cases) pressure from others not to. And my 50-odd current clients, whom I've been working with and—no surprise—having fun with for an average of about seven years each.

Also, speaking of fifth-grade math homework, remember that fifth-grade math teacher I dedicated the book to? Since we're in the acknowledgments now, I should acknowledge what a few of you probably already noticed in the Heartfelt Dedication, which is that the Heartfelt Dedication did not mention the name of the person to whom the book is heartfeltedly dedicated. Truth be told, that was because I couldn't remember it. And here we are, more than 200 self-indulgently overwritten pages later, and I still can't remember it. This may be the only book in history in which the author forgot the name of the Heartfelt Dedicatee.